PUBLIC ACCESS
TELEVISION

PUBLIC ACCESS
TELEVISION

America's Electronic Soapbox

Laura R. Linder

Foreword by Douglas Kellner

PRAEGER

Westport, Connecticut
London

Library of Congress Cataloging-in-Publication Data

Linder, Laura R.
  Public access television : America's electronic soapbox / Laura R.
  Linder ; foreword by Douglas Kellner.
      p. cm.
  Includes bibliographical references and index.
  ISBN 0–275–96487–6 (alk. paper). — ISBN 0–275–96488–4 (pbk. :
  alk. paper)
  1. Public-access television—United States—History. 2. Cable
television—Access—United States—History. I. Title.
  HE8700.72.U6L56 1999
  384.55′532—dc21   98–56631

British Library Cataloguing-in-Publication Data is available.

Library of Congress Catalog Card Number: 98–56631
ISBN: 0–275–96487–6
        0–275–96488–4 (pbk.)

First published in 1999

Praeger Publishers, 88 Post Road West, Westport, CT 06881
An imprint of Greenwood Publishing Group, Inc.
www.praeger.com

Printed in the United States of America

The paper used in this book complies with the
Permanent Paper Standard issued by the National
Information Standards Organization (Z39.48–1984).

10 9 8 7 6 5 4 3 2 1

For my son, Patrick M. Kirkman.
Anything is possible if you work toward it and believe.

Contents

List of Figures and Tables

Foreword

Public access television has been one of the most exciting and controversial developments in the intersection between media and democracy within the past several decades. Beginning in the 1970s, cable systems began to offer access channels to the public, so that groups and individuals could make programs for members of their own communities. Access systems began to proliferate and access programming that is now being cablecast regularly in such places as New York, Los Angeles, Boston, Chicago, Atlanta, Madison, Urbana, Austin, Greensboro, and perhaps as many as 4,000 other towns or regions of the country.

When cable television was widely introduced in the early 1970s, the Federal Communications Commission mandated that "beginning in 1972, new cable systems (and after 1977, all cable systems) in the 100 largest television markets be required to provide channels for government, for educational purposes, and most importantly, for public access." This mandate suggested that cable systems should make available three public access channels to be used for state and local government, education, and community public access use. "Public access" was construed to mean that the cable company should make available equipment and air time so that literally anybody could make noncommercial use of the access channel, and say and do anything that they wished, on a first-come, first-served basis, subject only to obscenity and libel laws. The result was an entirely different sort of programming, reflecting the interests of groups and individuals usually excluded from mainstream television.

The rationale for public access television was that, as mandated by the Federal Communications Act of 1934, the airwaves belong to the people, that in a democratic society it is useful to multiply public participation in political discussion, and that mainstream television severely limited the range of views and opinion. Public access television, then, would open television to the public; it would make possible community participation, and thus would be in the public interest of strengthening democracy.

Laura Linder's study provides one of the best histories available of the background of public access television—its regulatory history, philosophical justification, its current status, funding sources, and future. In this clearly written, accessible, and well-documented study, Linder examines the roots of public access television in discussions of public broadcasting in the United States, alternative media projects in Canada, and the development of alternative media centers in the United States and elsewhere. Linder discloses how U.S. government and regulatory agencies both enabled and weakened public access and examines in detail the funding of public access and some exemplary projects. She also discusses some of the more controversial access projects and programming and the ways that it can aid citizen involvement in public affairs and media debate.

As we enter a new high-tech era, it is extremely helpful to understand the attempts to democratize media of the past and Linder's study provides a useful overview of the history and potentials of public access television. In the midst of a great technological revolution, the future of access is uncertain. Linder documents some important contributions to democratic communications of the past and argues for the continued importance of public access television in the future. Whether a more democratic communications system emerges or dissolves is up to citizens who are interested in communicating with other citizens and nourishing instruments of democratic communication such as public access television. Present trends toward concentration of media ownership, commercialization, and tabloidization threaten the integrity of the public sphere and the possibilities for democratic communication. If our democracy is to survive and thrive we need to use all instruments of democratic communication such as community radio, public access television, and now the Internet. Linder informs us of the vibrant history and continuing potential of public access television. Her work will hopefully focus scholarly attention and activist intervention in this vital but often ignored domain of people's media.

Los Angeles, March 1999.

Douglas Kellner
Graduate School of Education
Moore Hall Mailbox 951521
UCLA
Los Angeles, CA 90095

kellner@ucla.edu
Fax: 310-206-6293
Phone: 310-825-0977

Preface

I became interested in public access television in 1989 when my friend Sol Jacobs told me about his experiences and frustrations with public access television in Greensboro, North Carolina. In listening to his stories, I began to understand his enthusiasm for public access television as well as its value. This book is the culmination of almost ten years of involvement in the local and national public access television movement, and the concern I share with many others about the future of this community communication tool—America's electronic soapbox. In order for the reader to understand my personal involvement, a brief history of public access television in Greensboro is necessary.

Greensboro is a city with a population of approximately two hundred thousand located in the Piedmont region of North Carolina. The path that the city took to public access television was long and winding, with many twists and turns. While the specifics of the journey are unique to Greensboro, the process has much in common with other locales.

The system of cable lines that brought cable television service to Greensboro was built by the Southern Bell Corporation in the mid-1960s. At that time, cable television was regarded by the public primarily as a means of assuring clear reception by eliminating airwave interference. Cable companies recognized that local franchises could be lucrative, but only because they saw cable television as a growth market. No one seemed to be thinking in terms of the potential for gaining direct access to people's living rooms with new or different programming.[1]

As early as 1966, when Southern Bell was still laying their lines, Jefferson Standard Broadcasting, a subsidiary of the Jefferson-Pilot Corporation, a large insurance provider and one of Greensboro's foremost corporate citizens, put in a bid to operate a community antenna television (CATV) system in Greensboro. Instead of building their own cable network, Jefferson-Pilot Corporation sought a lease agreement with Southern Bell to operate the fledgling cable system, Cablevision of Greensboro. Outbidding a local competitor, Vuemore Cablevision,

Inc., Jefferson-Carolina, as the new subsidiary was called, assumed operation of Cablevision in 1966.[2]

By mid-1967, with four hundred fifty miles of cable in place, Cablevision had begun to provide service to its first subscribers. But this progress was halted later that same year when, in an effort to prevent media monopolies, the Federal Communications Commission (FCC) put a nationwide freeze on all new cable construction where local systems were owned by telephone companies. This legal impasse lasted until 1972, when Cablevision was acquired by American Television and Communications Corporation (ATC), based in Englewood, Colorado. At the time there were approximately five thousand subscribers. But even with the legal barriers removed and a steady increase in the number of subscribers, the recession of 1973–1974 prevented greater expansion of cable during this time.[3]

Throughout this incipient period, Greensboro citizens expressed no apparent desire for, or knowledge of, public access television. This might have remained the case indefinitely except for a change in federal law. In 1972, the FCC made it mandatory for local cable operators in the largest one hundred television markets to provide three access channels, one for government, one for education, and one for public access television. Although Greensboro by itself would have been too small to fall under the guidelines, the FCC considered the Triad as a whole (including Winston-Salem and High Point) when designating market size, and the Triad market was one of the one hundred largest in the country.[4]

Ready to take advantage of this opportunity were two local activists, Jim Clark and Sol Jacobs. They founded a nonprofit organization called Community Access Television for the purpose of developing local programming. For several months in 1974 and 1975 Jacobs hosted a weekly talk show out of a makeshift studio behind the Cablevision offices. According to Clark, "with his grandfatherly smile and whiskery eyebrows, Jacobs emerged as the Walter Cronkite of Greensboro." Community Access Television fostered other programs as well, including a satiric show called "Plankton Playhouse," one episode of which, called "Jowls," was about a white killer pig that terrorized Greensboro. Clark referred to it as a "foul-smelling hit."[5]

Jacobs and Clark were not the only ones who were energized by the prospect of developing their own television programs. Saturday morning training sessions attracted dozens of individuals and groups representing diverse segments of the community. Seeking to raise the level of professionalism, local photographer Ira Blaustein organized a group of students into a production team called Photopharm Television Group. Most of the students were eighth and ninth graders who had been producing a news show over the school's closed circuit television system.[6]

In 1975, Jacobs helped to organize several meetings regarding public access television. These meetings culminated in a panel discussion that was cablecast from the Cablevision studios. The format for the program included an explanation of all four types of cable access channels—public, education, government, and leased—after which panelists fielded questions from viewers on an open telephone line. This was the first time such a show had taken place on public access television in Greensboro. But constant equipment breakdowns and lack of support from Cablevision were beginning to take their toll, and many would-be producers were discouraged. In a final attempt to revive Community Access Television, Jacobs asked the Greensboro City Council for $15,000 to purchase new equipment. "The cameras are so bad we can't get a picture suitable for broadcasting," he told them.[7] The request was denied.

The topic of public access television was not raised again until 1979 when the franchise agreement between Cablevision and the City of Greensboro came up for renewal and the negotiations became a matter of much public debate. An increase in demand for cable, fueled by the advent of the Home Box Office movie channel, combined with Cablevision's poor track record of service and caused the city council to take a tough public negotiating position. The City required Cablevision to post a $100,000 performance bond. In a council meeting, Mayor Jim Melvin referred to a "gross negligence of service"[8] and said that "next to dogs, Cablevision generates more citizen complaints than any other subject."[9]

But this "tough stance" did not translate into support for public access television. This became evident when Clark and Jacobs tried to convince the city council to add public access television services to the provisions in their contract with Cablevision. They cited the 1978 report *Cable Television in North Carolina*, published by the North Carolina Center for Public Policy Research, in which the potential of public access television was illustrated and examples of quality programming from around the country were described. As a model, Clark and Jacobs noted that the City of Durham had required Cablevision of Durham to supply a studio, cameras, and technical assistance for community groups as part of their franchise agreement. They also pointed to an internal City of Greensboro staff recommendation that a public access channel be provided as soon as Cablevision's capacity allowed, estimated to be around 1984. "They just weren't interested," said Clark.[10] The new fifteen-year franchise agreement that the City of Greensboro signed with Cablevision in 1979 contained no additional requirements regarding public access television. Existing access service, poor at best, was doomed to limp along until 1994.

Among those who did seize the opportunity for television exposure, the most clearly identifiable group were the African-American churches. Looking for ways to deliver their sermons to shut-ins, potential members, and the general public, local African-American ministers quickly discovered that public access television was an inexpensive way to expand their ministries beyond the church walls. They found independent producers who would videotape their services and cablecast them on the public access channel. But few in Greensboro utilized public access television for the civic purposes for which it had been created, and the dream of public access television as a means of broadening the "marketplace of ideas" went into hibernation. Neither the franchiser (the City of Greensboro) nor the franchisee (Cablevision) seemed to care.

But Sol Jacobs had not given up. He had broadened support for public access television in Greensboro through Citizens for Responsible Government (CFRG), a progressive organization he had founded with his brothers, Cy and Morry. He knew that the next opportunity for improving access would come with the 1994 franchise renegotiations and that the lobbying effort needed to begin well in advance. In his eighties and in frail health, he recruited Sally Alvarez and me to carry the public access television banner. In 1991, we began talking to city council members about the opportunity that the renegotiations afforded us to obtain public access television services for the citizens of Greensboro. We were abetted in our lobbying efforts by Carolyn Allen, then a city councilwoman, who had also been a founding member of Citizens for Responsible Government.

In July of 1991, we sent out a letter under the auspices of Citizens for Responsible Government to a list of individuals and organizations we thought might (or should) be interested in public access television. The letter provided basic information regarding public access television and the upcoming contract renegotiations, and invited recipients to attend an informational meeting at the public library in August. Only nine people attended, but they represented Guilford Technical Community College, the Family Life Council, and other organizations, as well as independent producers. The brainstorming at this session helped us to formulate a strategy for promoting public access television in Greensboro. We were also compiling a growing mailing list of access supporters. At our next meeting we named ourselves Greensboro Citizens Cable Advisory Committee (GCCAC).

As a result of much educating, lobbying, and networking, contract talks took on a very different aspect than they had in 1979. In 1991, the City hired a national consulting company for guidance in the renegotiation process. The following year, three citizen task forces were appointed by the city council to gather information and make recommendations about public, educational, and governmental access. Heeding the advice of GCCAC and CFRG, the city also created an office to oversee the renegotiations process.

Later that year, the City of Greensboro sponsored a cable television seminar to determine the future of public access television programming. The consultants presented the national perspective on PEG access and showed a videotape sampler of public access television programming. This was a turning point. Seeing samples of high quality access programs was a key factor in gaining support from city council and staff, and inspiring GCCAC members to educate others about the potential for access in Greensboro.

In February 1992, the city began conducting a community assessment to study the services and programming that cable television can and should offer area residents, institutions, and organizations in the future. At the same time, the consultants were conducting a mail survey, asking representatives from government agencies, educational institutions, and community organizations to describe their current usage of public access television and to forecast future usage. The return rate was 77 percent (fifty-one surveys out of sixty-six), and the information proved to be valuable in articulating citizen needs and perceptions.[11]

The assessment, the survey, and the reports from the three task forces enabled the city to identify the following community needs related to public access television: channels for public, educational, and governmental access, and additional channels if needed in the future; training and production assistance; studio, portable, and postproduction equipment and facilities; selected program origination points to be designated for cablecasting; and interconnection with nearby communities. This list of needs formed the basis of the Request for Proposal (RFP) that the city was preparing to send to Cablevision to begin the formal renegotiation process.[12]

Negotiations between the City of Greensboro and Cablevision began in earnest in 1993 and continued through 1994. Public access television again became a matter of public debate in 1994 between Carolyn Allen, who was elected mayor in 1993, and former city councilman Tom Phillips, who would run unsuccessfully against Allen in the mayoral campaign the following year. Since Cablevision had the option of passing along much of the franchise fee in the form of higher subscriber rates, Phillips portrayed it as a "tax." He also capitalized on the controversy created by the cablecasting of a program on the public access channel that featured nudity and foul language. The show had been cablecast in the early evening by Cablevision and was greeted with howls of protest from parents and others in the community who thought the show was not appropriate to air when children might be watching.

Coverage in the local media during this time was extensive and frequently damaging to the promotion of public access television. The issues of cost and offensive programming threatened to overshadow the benefits of having a community communication outlet on local television. But with the help of Citizens for Responsible Government, we were prepared for a long-term campaign and were able to counteract most of the negative publicity.

When the franchise agreement was finally signed in January 1995 (retroactive to October 1994 when the previous contract had expired), it stipulated that public access television would be managed and operated by a nonprofit corporation; educational access would be operated by a consortium of local schools, colleges, and universities; and governmental access would be managed by the City of Greensboro. The following June, Sally Alvarez and I were appointed, by the city council, along with sixteen other people, to a board of directors whose assigned task was to set up the nonprofit corporation and take over the operation of the public access channel. Greensboro Community Television (GCTV), the new nonprofit organization, was guaranteed startup money and modest operating funds for the duration of the ten-year contract.

By the spring and summer of 1996, GCTV had hired the necessary staff, including an executive director, Karen Toering, who had extensive public access television experience in Wisconsin and Indiana. With the official takeover of the channel scheduled for October, the challenge was to upgrade the image of public access television. The access channel had previously been a hodgepodge of commercial programming, a few shows generated by the local school system, church-based shows, city council meetings, and a motley assortment of vanity video performers.

With the help of Toering and the GCTV staff and board members, we developed a plan. A slogan was adopted—"A New Face for Cable 8"—and a public relations campaign was launched. A launch committee was formed and a public relations consultant was hired to help plan an opening event.[13]

A media campaign was undertaken in order to set the stage for the opening and do damage control on the negative view of public access television that had previously dominated local media coverage. A media kit was designed, including press releases, fact sheets, a poster, biographies, timeline, and a brochure. Toering began to appear regularly on talk shows and before civic organizations to introduce herself and the "new" cable channel 8.

After soliciting applications from more than one hundred nonprofit organizations, GCTV staff selected ten and facilitated the production of programs based on their activities. The purpose was to air high-quality programming that reflected the community in the first weeks after the takeover. The organizations for whom programs were produced were the Epilepsy Association, the Jaycees, Urban Ministry, the Greensboro Sports Commission, the Volunteer Center, Uplift, Inc., the Junior League, the Piedmont Blues Preservation Society, the Humane Society, and the Community Theater of Greensboro.

A series of three creative promotional spots were created for GCTV by University of North Carolina at Greensboro film students and an agreement was secured whereby the spots were run on cable channel 8 and other Cablevision channels in the weeks leading up to the launch. A thirty-minute video introduction to the channel, using the title "A New Face for Cable 8," was produced. The video featured a brief history of public access television in Greensboro, introduced board members, toured the new facility, and explained the philosophy behind public access television and what GCTV hoped to do in the future.

The GCTV facility was officially opened in October 1996 with much fanfare. As part of the grand opening festivities, Mayor Allen broke open a bottle of prop champagne over a television set in front of the new facility, in downtown Greensboro. The entire grand opening celebration was cablecast live on the public access channel. At this point, Greensboro became one of only six active public access television operations in the state (the others were in Raleigh, Charlotte, Chapel Hill, Boone, and Durham).

By October 1998, more than 450 organizations and individuals were paid members of Greensboro Community Television. GCTV was averaging 141 new shows per month and, in what is perhaps the best indicator of success, over two thousand hours of facility and equipment use per month. Some of the continuing shows that have appeared on GCTV include "Nashville Strokes," a country music show; "AAP," an interview program featuring representatives from the local African-American community; "Staying Healthy," a local health and exercise program; "Reel Tyme Video Countdown," a music show featuring rhythm and blues, reggae, jazz, and artist interviews; "Kidfest," a dance show for children six to twelve years of age; "Legislative News Update," featuring news from the North Carolina General Assembly; and "Wild and Wonderful," a monthly show from the North Carolina Zoo. One-time shows have appeared on such topics as land use, elder care, financial planning, and water quality. A weekly public affairs program, entitled "Democracy in Action," was dedicated to the memory of Sol Jacobs.

While the Greensboro journey is unique, the obstacles faced by local access advocates are similar to those encountered in other locales. The public discourse may have been more proscribed and the political climate more conservative than in other parts of the country, but the basic issues—public participation, free speech, the terms of the franchise agreement, controversial programming—are common to all such efforts.

In every location where people are trying to establish public access television or where public access television currently exists, there is always the threat that it will not be funded or that the funding will be inadequate. Describing the background and current status of public access television in the United States, discussing the nature of that underfunding and nonfunding threat, and offering methods for mitigation, are the goals of this book. The chapters that follow offer an overall view of public access television in the United States and recommendations toward securing the future of our electronic soapbox.

NOTES

1. John Roberts, "Cablevision Plans Major Expansion," *Greensboro (North Carolina) Record*, 28 March 1979, sec. A, p. 1, 5.

2. Application for Permit to City Council of City of Greensboro (North Carolina), May 12, 1996. Early cable television systems were called community antenna television since that was all they were—large antennae on top of tall towers, hills, or mountains to improve reception with lines going to nearby homes.

3. Roberts, "Cablevision Plans Major Expansion," sec. A, p. 5.

4. John Roberts, "Cable: Quality Programming is Necessary," *Greensboro (North Carolina) Record*, 30 March 1979, sec. A, p. 1, 10.

5. Jim Clark, "Revolt in Videoland," *Triad (North Carolina)* 4, no. 1 (winter 1979), 18.

6. Bill Lee, "Team Approach Lets Access TV Look Professional," *Greensboro (North Carolina) Daily News*, 21 February 1975, sec. B, p. 1.

7. Quoted in Lindsey Gruson, "Cablevision to Post Bond, to Install Public Access," Greensboro (North Carolina) Daily News, 12 April 1979, sec. C, p. 1.

8. John Roberts, "Cablevision: Local Government Decides CG Fate," *Greensboro (North Carolina)* Record, 29 March 1979, sec. A, p. 1.

9. Winston Cavin, "City Council Blasts 'Sorry' Cable TV," *Greensboro (North Carolina) Daily News*, 7 March 1979, sec. B, p. 1.

10. "Cable Television in North Carolina," N.C. Center for Public Policy Research, Inc., Raleigh, NC, 1978, 30–45; "Cable and the Public," *Greensboro (North Carolina) Daily*

News, 12 April 1979, sec. A, p. 4; and Roberts, "Cable: Quality Programming is Necessary," sec. A, p. 1.

11. *City of Greensboro Cable Task Force Report*, City of Greensboro, NC, September 1992, 73.

12. Ibid., 1.

13. Sally Alvarez, "Building Community Support," *Community Media Review* (Spring 1997): 9.

Acknowledgments

I would like to thank the following people for all their help in getting this book published: Mildred Graham Vasan, my editor, and James T. Sabin, editor at Greenwood Publishing, for the opportunity to bring the book to fruition; Douglas Kellner and William E. Knox for reading the manuscript and offering solid suggestions; Jeremy Byman and Lynn Hamilton for reading earlier versions; Nancy C. Fogarty, Assistant Reference Librarian at University of North Carolina at Greensboro, for her wise counsel; both Sally M. Alvarez and Whitney Grove Vanderwerff for providing me with remarkable role models, ongoing encouragement, and support; my longtime friend and mentor, John L. Jellicorse, for offering encouragement whenever I needed it—his belief in me helped me believe in myself; John R. Bittner, for his counsel, patience, and direction—without his guidance, I would not be where I am today. The memory of Sol Jacobs' optimism and his vision of what public access could be acted as a beacon to help keep me focused. My father, James B. Linder, and my mother, Gene H. Linder, have been my biggest champions through the years. Without the support and love of these people, I would have been unable to achieve all I have accomplished.

To my husband, Gary S. Kenton, to whom I owe so much, I give my undying love and gratitude. His love, faith, and support as well as his unending patience for reading and rereading this work helped me to be a better thinker, researcher, and writer.

Introduction

Between 1983 and 1996, ownership of major media outlets in the United States shrank from fifty national and multinational corporations to ten. The majority of all the media is owned by these ten corporations. As Ben Bagdikian states in the preface to the fifth edition of his *Media Monopoly*, "[T]his handful of giants has created what is, in effect, a new communications cartel within the United States."[1] As ownership of the mass media has become increasingly concentrated, two problems have emerged. The first is a further narrowing and homogenization of the range of opinions that are disseminated by the mass media; the second, which follows from the first, is decreasing coverage of local issues. A potential counterforce to both of these problems is public access television. This book is an attempt to show how public access television has addressed and can address these problems, and to identify key factors that will affect the continuation of public access television in the future.[2]

Concentrated ownership has also meant greater media commercialization. Commercial mass media in the United States are in business to make money, and therefore must maximize the number of consumers exposed to sponsors' advertisements. Thus, there is a strong incentive to make media messages as entertaining as possible to attract as many consumers as possible to attract as many advertisers as possible.[3] Accordingly, in the search for the largest audience, media tend to emphasize general interest, lightweight, or sensationalistic fare to the exclusion of meaningful local issues. Audiences for more meaningful types of programming are often considered too small to deliver desirable demographics and an adequate market share. In their quest for the largest audience, most media tend to omit or marginalize the people who are not in the broadest majority audience.[4]

Media consumers are rarely given the opportunity to hear voices not sponsored or influenced by corporate ownership or to disseminate their own messages. Ordinary people with something to say have few outlets. The only section of most magazines and newspapers devoted to undiluted and unedited public opinion is the letters to the editor page, yet only a small percentage of letters received by newspapers and magazines are published. Another possible outlet for individual dissemination of information is the Internet, but the skills and equipment necessary to create the message limit access. In addition, the audience for Internet messages is too diverse geographically to be of benefit for localized community messages. Broadcasting offers talk radio as a potential outlet, but this forum operates in much the same way as letters to the editor, in that callers are screened first and only a few are permitted access to the airwaves. The film industry has no equivalent to the letters to the editor page.

It is always possible for individuals to print their own newspapers or magazines, but distribution is generally a prohibitive logistical and financial obstacle. It is the rare, independently wealthy individual who is able to distribute widely enough to approach the number of readers necessary to publish a viable newspaper or magazine. So, even as the electronic media have become increasingly dominant as purveyors of ideas, the means of production in broadcasting and film have become prohibitively expensive, beyond the means of all but a handful of corporations.

The importance of mass media in public discourse in our society, and the special role that public access has the potential to play, was acknowledged by Supreme Court Justices Kennedy and Ginsburg in 1996. "Minds are not changed in streets and parks as they once were," the judges wrote, "To an increasing degree, the more significant interchanges of ideas and shaping of public consciousness occur in mass and electronic media."[5]

The maintenance of a free press was important to the founders of the United States because of their prior experience with interference and domination under British rule. But the founders were equally passionate about freedom of speech and the importance of the free flow of ideas. The Supreme Court reiterated this importance in its landmark decision upholding the Fairness Doctrine, *Red Lion Broadcasting v. FCC*: "*It is the right of the viewers and listeners, not the right of the broadcasters, which is paramount* . . . it is the purpose of the First Amendment to preserve an uninhibited marketplace of ideas in which truth will ultimately prevail, rather than to countenance monopolization of that market." [Italics added.][6]

The founders of this country recognized three important tenets as they adopted the principles of democracy. First, they understood that an effective democracy requires an active, informed citizenry and a free exchange of ideas. Second, they recognized that active participation by itself was no guarantee of outcomes that were beneficial to the long-term interests of the republic. For citizen involvement to have a salutary effect, the citizens must be privy to a broad range of information and opinions. Only after being exposed to all the alternatives can the average citizen make educated decisions regarding public policy. Third, the founders understood that for the citizenry to be broadly informed, it was necessary to protect the free flow of ideas. While they would hardly recognize the delivery systems that dominate contemporary media, these basic tenets remain.

How can there be "an uninhibited marketplace of ideas" without the means or without the access? On one hand, we have a doctrine of fairness and openness articulated by the Constitution and the courts, and, on the other hand, an information delivery system that is more concerned with ratings and revenues than with debate and discourse.

Considerable attention has been focused on freedom of the press, and broadcasters have devoted a great deal of energy and money to its defense. But the corporate interests that dominate media ownership have generally marshalled the resources that have been brought to bear. Because of the concentration of ownership of mass media in the United States, citizens often lack access to the multitude of viewpoints that exist in their own communities. Although there are an increasing number of specialized magazines and a profusion of "narrowcast" cable channels (for example, the History, Golf, and Weather Channels), the messages being disseminated through these media are, for the most part, being developed by media managers and their corporate, commercial agents, and are targeted to a larger, albeit specialized, national audience.[7] As Douglas Kellner states in *Television and the Crisis of Democracy*, "In a commercial broadcasting system . . . commerce predominates over communication and the private interests of advertisers and broadcasters systematically prevail over the public interest and democracy."[8] How can people speak and hear noncommercial, localized voices and ideas when the majority of the media outlets are controlled by a few megacorporations? Public access television represents a significant response to this problem. With the advent of public access television, the public has been provided the practical means of disseminating its messages in its communities, as well as receiving the messages of others, through the dominant medium of television that had heretofore served only commercial interests. As part of its mission, for example, Chicago Access Network (CAN TV) specifically addresses the "public's right to communicate to others through TV."[9]

Although cable television has been available in the United States for almost fifty years, public access to cable television has existed for little more than half that time. Since it began, somewhat tentatively, in the early 1970s, public access television has developed in three primary areas: public, educational, and governmental. Public access television is programming produced by and for the general public. Educational access refers to access programming produced by an educational institution such as public school, community college, or university. Governmental access is programming produced by governmental agencies, including city councils, fire and police departments, and health departments, among others. These three types of access are referred to collectively as PEG access.[10]

PUBLIC ACCESS TELEVISION DEFINED

Public access television, or community television, as it is frequently called, began as an "attempt to use television as a direct means of communication without interference from professional middlemen such as journalists, directors, and producers."[11] Other descriptions of public access television include "programming by third parties other than the cable operators and the programmers they select";[12] a "unique opportunity to express . . . ideas and to convey information to members of the community";[13] "the production and distribution of programming by the public, municipal agencies, institutions, and similar organizations made available without charge";[14] "an electronic forum where all interested citizens can appear before their community to share information, discuss ideas, record local events, and entertain";[15] and the "video equivalent of the speaker's soap box or . . . the printed leaflet."[16]

For our purposes, there is a denser but more functional definition of public access television. Public access television consists of people not affiliated with the cable operator, using their own equipment or equipment provided to them by the cable operator or local government at no or minimal cost, to produce noncommercial television shows that are cablecast over a channel that is provided, at no cost, solely for public access television. Public access television enables people to disseminate their messages to a local television audience, without the content being edited, filtered, or altered. And for minorities this is especially important. As Jesikah Maria Ross and J. Aaron Spitzer state in their article "Public Access Television: the Message, the Medium, and the Movement," for *Art Papers*, public access television "fosters greater cultural participation by offering cultural minorities the opportunity to represent themselves the way they choose to be represented, rather than through the eyes of commercial stations which often value good teeth and accentless pronunciation above a commitment to incorporating diversity into their brief bursts of airtime between advertisements."[17]

A review of the rationale put forth by public access television proponents reveals five key underlying objectives:

1. To create community by providing the means for individuals and groups to express their ideas and messages in video form, and disseminate them to the public.

2. to empower people by demystifying the television production process and providing a form (video) and an outlet for their messages.

3. to encourage public discourse and diversity awareness.

4. to create a center where individuals and groups can interact and cooperate in the production of video programs.

5. to use film and video technology to bring about social change.

The television medium is predominantly privately owned and exclusive, with the general public most often relegated to the role of passive receivers. For democracy to function effectively, people need to be actively engaged with civic matters, and to do so effectively and constructively, they need to be aware of the diversity of opinions in their communities. They need to hear alternatives to the concentrated, commercial messages that dominate the mass media. But even more importantly, they need to become active citizens instead of passive receivers of others' messages. Public access television seeks to provide the means for people to create, distribute, and receive their own local, noncommercial messages via the medium of television.[18]

As early as 1972, in *United States v. Midwest Video Corp.*, the U.S. Supreme Court recognized cable television as an important outlet "for community self-expression" and as "one response to the increasing concentration of power over public discourse."[19] Three years later, after researching possible community uses of cable television, Pamela Doty stated in her essay in the *Journal of Communication*, "Public Access Cable TV: Who Cares?", that "The theoreticians of the public-access movement see public-access TV as the ideal vehicle of communication for a truly pluralistic, participatory society. More concretely, they see it as sparking a revival of local activism and community spirit by becoming a neighborhood communications center, enlarging upon the functions formerly performed by community newspapers."[20] Almost twenty-five years later, this vision of the potential for public access television remains alive but only marginally realized. Currently, there are an estimated two thousand public access centers in the United States producing more than fifteen thousand hours of original, locally focused programming every week.[21] But even as public access television has slowly developed and spread from community to community, changes in the telecommunications industry have raised potential threats to the public access television delivery system. After the deregulation of the cable industry in the 1980s, the telecommunications and electric power industries expressed a growing interest in entering the video delivery business; and with advances in direct broadcast satellite service, the future of public access television is uncertain.[22]

There are six steps that would enable public access television to continue to fulfill its role as our electronic soapbox. One would be to increase public understanding of and participation in public access television. Without increased public awareness there will be little or no support, and without public participation there is little reason for such support to exist.

The second step to ensure the continuation of public access television would be for public access television operators to become financially self-sufficient. Most public access television organizations receive the majority of their financial support from their local cable company and/or their local governing body through the franchise agreement negotiated by those two parties. A small part of public access television budgets comes from membership fees,[23] equipment rentals, and private sources. The incentive to secure financial autonomy would seem to be greater in this fast-changing regulatory and technological environment. A part of becoming self-sufficient would be for public access television centers to map out a comprehensive fund raising plan.

A third step would be to increase media literacy at the national, state, and local levels. People who understand how the media work would be better able to understand the importance of public access television. Media literacy needs to be encouraged in schools as well as through nonprofit organizations and workshops. These workshops could be cosponsored by the local public access center and then cablecast over the public access channel.

A fourth step would be for each public access television center and its supporters to become members of the Alliance for Community Media. This professional organization offers important information and support that are necessary for maintaining the capability and resolve of a public access television center, staff, board members, and activists, and gives centers a voice in advocating for regulatory reforms at the national level.

A fifth step would be for public access television centers to create and maintain a good relationship with their funding sources. Working with local cable companies, especially, could ultimately help the cable industry understand the importance and value of public access television to their community and to its economic well-being.

A final step would be for public access television advocates and supporters to work at the federal, state, and local levels to require all other companies providing similar video delivery services to adhere to the rules and regulations that currently apply to cable companies. Some local governments have already written ordinances to require any video delivery service to adhere to the current cable rules and regulations, and with the passage of the 1996 Telecommunications Act, Congress extended the existing public access cable television regulations to other providers of video services. However, it is still too early to see how this regulation may be necessary and, if it is, whether it will be enforced. These six steps outline the factors that need to be addressed to assure the continuation of the electronic soapbox into the twenty-first century. A model illustrating the six areas is shown in Figure 1.

In this era of telecommunication expansion into video delivery, direct broadcast satellite, and wireless cable service,[24] the security of public access television is by

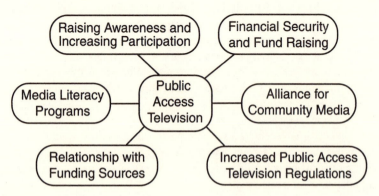

Figure 1
Factors Affecting the Future of Public Access Television

no means assured. This book proposes to address the future of public access television by addressing the above areas of concern. Chapters 1 to 3 provide background information by reviewing the history, regulations, and current status of public access television. Chapter 4 explains the current funding mechanisms of public access television and provides a discussion of responses from public access television centers about their funding sources and fund raising practices. The final chapter interprets these responses in light of the history, regulations, and current status of public access television, and offers recommendations for ensuring the future of the electronic soapbox into the twenty-first century. For, as George Gerbner has said, "Those who control the stories of a culture, control the culture."[25]

NOTES

1. Ben H. Bagdikian, *The Media Monopoly.* 5th ed. (Boston: Beacon, 1992), ix, xiii.

2. See, e.g., Pat Aufderheide, "150 Channels and Nothin' On," *The Progressive* 56 (1992): 36; Bagdikian, xxviii–xxx, 45; J. P. Coustel, "New Rules for Cable Television in the USA: Reducing the Market Power of Cable Operators," *Telecommunications Policy* (April 1993): 205; Peter Dahlgren, *Television and the Public Sphere: Citizenship, Democracy, and the Media.* (London: Sage Publications, 1995), 1–2; Ralph Engelman, *Public Radio and Television in America: A Political History* (Thousand Oaks, CA: Sage Publications, 1996), 287–89; Douglas Kellner, *Television and the Crisis of Democracy* (Boulder, CO: Westview, 1990), 80–81; and Rick Szykowny, "The Threat of Public Access: An Interview with Chris Hill and Brian Springer," *The Humanist* 54 (1994): 15–16.

3. See, e.g., Bagdikian, 8; Dahlgren, 148; Kellner, 78–79; Michael Morgan, "Television and Democracy" in *Cultural Politics in Contemporary America*, ed. Ian Angus and Sut Jhally (New York: Routledge, 1989), 252–53.

4. See, e.g., Nicholas Garnham, "The Media and the Public Sphere," *Intermedia* (January 1986): 28; Kellner, 9; James Lull, *Media, Communication, Culture* (New York: Columbia University, 1995), 36; Morgan, 246; Szykowny, 15.

5. *Denver Area Education Telecommunications Consortium* v. FCC, 116 S. Ct. 2374 (1996) No. 95–124, 132.

6. *Red Lion Broadcasting, Inc. v. FCC*, 395 US 367 (1969). The Fairness Doctrine, first articulated by the FCC in 1949, mandated broadcasters spend a percentage of their time discussing different sides of public interest issues in their community. It was added to Section 315 of the *Communication Act of 1934* in 1959 and in 1967 personal attack rules and political editorializing guidelines were added. The Fairness Doctrine was abolished by the FCC in 1985.

7. See e.g., Bagdikian, 4; Kellner, 94.

8. Kellner, 95.

9. Bert Briller, "Accent on Access Television," *Television Quarterly* 28, no. 2 (Spring 1996): 54.

10. Deborah George, "The Cable Communications Policy Act of 1984 and Content Regulation of Cable Television," *New England Law Review* 20, no. 4 (1984–85): 779–804; and Ralph Engelman, "The Origins of Public Access Cable Television 1966–1972," *Journalism Monographs* 23 (October 1990): 1.

11. Ibid.

12. Michael I. Meyerson, "Cable Television's New Legal Universe: Early Judicial Response to the Cable Act," *Cardozo Arts and Entertainment Law Journal* 6 (1987): 1–36.

13. George, 783.

14. John Journal Copelan, Jr. and A. Quinn Jones, III, "Cable Television, Public Access and Local Governments," *Entertainment and Sports Law Journal* 1 (1984): 37–51.

15. Joyce Miller, "The Development of Community Television," *Community Television Review* 9 (1986): 12.

16. H.R. Rep. No. 934, 98th Cong., 2nd Sess. 55, reprinted in *1984 U.S. Code Congressional and Administration News*, 4655.

17. Jesikah Maria Ross and J. Aaron Spitzer, "Public Access Television: The Message, the Medium, and the movement," *Art Papers* 18, no. 3 (May/June 1994): 3, 43.

18. Greg Boozell, "What's Wrong with Public Access Television?" *Art Papers* 17, no. 4 (July/August 1993): 7.

19. David Ehrenfest Steinglass, "Extending *Pruneyard*: Citizens' Right to Demand Public Access Cable Channels," *New York University Law Review* 71 (October 1996): 1160.

20. Pamela Doty, "Public Access Cable Television: Who Cares?" *Journal of Communication* 25, (1975): 33–41.

21. Briller, 51.

22. Direct broadcast satellite (DBS) service is the transmission of an array of channels via television signal by satellite to the individual subscriber's home. Subscribers must buy a small receiving dish and pay a monthly fee. The two major DBS service providers supply over seventy video channels (including most, if not all, channels currently provided by cable) and fourteen to thirty-two audio channels. However, subscribers must have a separate antenna or basic cable service to receive local broadcast stations.

23. Most public access facilities require producers to become members of the facility. The membership fee is usually ten to fifty dollars per year, on a sliding scale, and encourages producers to respect the facility and equipment, and to feel a sense of commitment towards the station. Members usually receive free training classes, a monthly newsletter, and representation on the board of directors, if one exists.

24. Wireless cable, or Multichannel Multipoint Distribution Service (MMDS), as it is more technically known, provides a array of channels like wired cable, to subscribers via microwave signal.

25. Quoted in Laurel M. Church, "Community Access Television: What We Don't Know and Why We Don't Know It," *Journal of Film and Video* 39 (Summer 1987): 13.

1

History of Public Access Television

Public access television has existed in one form or another for more than twenty-five years. As with most innovations in communication, public access television did not spring from any single place or event. But the roots of contemporary public access television can be traced to two primary sources, both dating to the mid-1960s. The first was the passage of the Public Broadcasting Act by the United States Congress in 1967. The second was the advent of the National Film Board of Canada's service organization, Challenge for Change. These two developments created both the regulatory and philosophic environment in which public access television could germinate.

PUBLIC BROADCASTING ROOTS

The philosophic and legal foundation for public access television in the United States was embedded in the letter and the spirit of the Public Broadcasting Act of 1967. This legislation created the Corporation for Public Broadcasting (CPB), based in Washington, D.C. and funded by Congress. One of the first tasks of the CPB was to create the Public Broadcasting Service (PBS), a programming arm for this newly formed corporation. The CPB is primarily a funding organization, while PBS facilitates the production and acquisition of programming.

Two years after the formation of the Corporation for Public Broadcasting, the Public Broadcasting Service began broadcasting. Examples of early PBS programming include "The Great American Dream Machine," "an iconoclastic public affairs magazine," and "The 51st State," which covered the politics and culture of New York City. Although early PBS programming was innovative and sometimes controversial (as is public access television programming today), it was programming produced prior to the passage of the 1967 Act that better fit a progressive, "cutting edge" description.[1]

Created in 1966–1967, "Public Broadcasting Laboratory" (PBL) was one example of progressive, pre-CPB programming. Eric Barnouw described it in *The Image Empire: A History of Broadcasting in the United States Since 1953*: "Mindful of its function as an alternative voice, it dipped into the work of fringe theaters, cabarets, and underground films, and inevitably reflected the angry subculture. The thrust of the message was anti-war, anti-racist, anti-establishment."[2] Because of its increasing need to appeal to a broad cross section of the population and its financial ties to the government, later PBS programming proved to be less daring.

In 1970, the more than one hundred public broadcasting member stations throughout the country became a network. By 1972, this number had grown to 233. This national network gave PBS the potential for reaching a broad audience with noncommercial programs. But PBS was tentative in exercising this newly acquired power. There was a natural tension created between the desire of some PBS producers to create challenging and provocative programs on the one hand and the direct sponsorship by the government on the other. At the time, President Richard Nixon harbored a deep mistrust and resentment of the media, as did his vice president, Spiro Agnew, and top speech writer, William Safire. Their memorable description of the media as "nattering nabobs of negativism"[3] summed up this antagonistic relationship. When PBS aired programs such as "Banks and the Poor," a documentary that exposed regressive and discriminatory practices in the banking industry, the reaction of the administration and others on Capitol Hill was decidedly negative.[4]

Under considerable pressure from the White House and Congress, which was, after all, its funding source, public television offered less innovative and controversial programming in the early 1970s than it had in the pre-PBS years, but it was still different from network television fare. The survival of such high-profile programs as "Sesame Street," which debuted in November 1969, and "Nova," which first appeared in March 1974, may have as much to do with their relative lack of controversial subject matter as with their overall quality.[5] Control of PBS by the CPB (and hence the government), had the effect of assuring that PBS programming would be more mainstream and middle-of-the-road. There was always the tacit threat that funding could be curtailed or eliminated altogether.

In 1972, the Nixon Administration made good on these threats, vetoing a bill to authorize funding for CPB and PBS that had large margins of support in both houses. Because any future funding would depend on the restructuring of both the CPB and PBS, the bill dramatically changed the way the CPB viewed its role and brought what many consider to be the "golden era" of PBS to an end. The CPB was forced to turn increasingly to corporations for financial support. This greater reliance on the private sector for funding had a chilling effect on producers and administrators and resulted in less innovative, challenging programming.[6]

During these early years of public television, some public stations experimented with localized programming. "Catch 44," a regular half-hour show produced by WGBH Foundation in Boston, allowed local organizations an opportunity to speak out on television without cost. Other public television stations also began allowing time for the public on television. In Philadelphia a show of this type was titled "Take 12"; in Detroit, "Your Turn"; and in San Francisco, "Open Studio." But these early efforts did not survive the experimental stage. By the mid-1970s, none of the pioneer projects were still on the air. Although these shows were early examples of community television in the United States, public access television really got its start in Canada.[7]

CANADIAN ROOTS

A more grounded, focused movement toward community television was begun by the Canadian National Film Board in 1966. Challenge for Change (the English version) and Societé Nouvelle (the French version) were service organizations created "to help eradicate the causes of poverty by provoking basic social change" using film (and later video). George Stoney, guest executive director of Challenge for Change from 1968 to 1970, described the program as "a social contract between the people who were in charge of a government program—an agency or social service—and the people who were the recipients of that program or service, designed to find out how they felt about what was being done and what they would like to see changed."[8]

Challenge for Change was grounded in the social documentary tradition of John Grierson (*Drifters* [1929] and *Housing Problems* [1936]). This tradition was based on making films with people, not about them; and Challenge for Change took this idea one step farther and involved their subjects even more in the actual production of the films.[9]

One of the early successes of Challenge for Change was the Fogo Island Project. Fogo Island is a small community located off the northeast shore of Canada where the primary source of livelihood was the fishing industry. Because this industry was declining and more than half of the residents lived on welfare, the Canadian government was considering relocating the entire community of five thousand people. Although Fogo Island as a community was besieged and fragmented, Challenge for Change saw an opportunity to use "film as a social catalyst."[10]

The Fogo Islanders did not want to be relocated; however, they were unable to get their message across to government leaders, primarily because the various groups were so disparate. Not only were they unable to talk with the government officials, they had difficulty talking with one another. Challenge for Change saw its mission as one of facilitator, and its medium as film.

The Fogo Island Challenge for Change crew, headed by Colin Low, a senior producer at the National Film Board, took their equipment to Fogo and recruited islanders to talk about themselves, their lives, and their island. They also taught the islanders how to operate the equipment.

Intending to produce traditional social documentaries the team found that the islanders were more responsive when short films were made based on a single interview or event. Instead of being edited and interwoven with other footage and narrative, these shorts, 28 in all, were left largely intact. [They were] referred to . . . as linear chunks of reality. In the six hours of footage, subjects such as *Fishermen's Meeting*, *The Songs of Chris Cobb*, *The Children of Fogo Island*, and *Billy Crane Moves Away* offered a panorama of the people and problems of Fogo.[11]

By scheduling group showings of the films in various locations on the island, the films were used to create community and foster dialogue among the different groups on the island as well as helping them present their case to government officials. Ultimately, government plans to relocate the islanders were dropped.

In 1968, a major technological breakthrough occurred that altered how Challenge for Change went about its work and set the stage for public access television: portable video equipment was introduced by Sony Corporation. The "portapak" weighed only twenty pounds and did not require professionally trained directors, camera operators, or sound operators. Two other advantages were that the videotape could be reviewed immediately (film had to be sent off to be developed), and production costs were drastically reduced (in addition to developing expenses, labor intensive tasks such as sound synchronization were eliminated.)[12]

This greater convenience and flexibility in creating video coincided with another advance in technology: the rapid expansion of cable television. Cities across Canada were being wired for cable television, bringing opportunities for production and airing of localized programming. The people at Challenge for Change began to see a new outlet for their work in the expansion of the number of channels made available by cable television.

In 1970, the prototype for public access television was developed in Thunder Bay, Ontario. A local civic organization initiated a plan to operate a cable channel for the local community, relying on Challenge for Change to supply the equipment and train members of the community in its use. The group eventually cablecast locally produced community programming four hours a day. Shows were produced live as well as taped, and the important precedent of using half-inch video was established (half-inch video was not considered broadcast quality but was deemed acceptable for cablecasting). The Thunder Bay Community Program lasted less than a year, but it demonstrated the potential of public access television. Other public access television programs were also aided by Challenge for Change.

In 1971, after public hearings, the Canadian Radio and Television Commission issued its Policy Statement on Cable Television and required that public access be a comprehensive part of cable television development in Canada.[13] In the meantime, George Stoney moved to New York, spreading the seeds of public access television to the United States.

THE ALTERNATE MEDIA CENTER

Upon his return to the United States in 1971, Stoney, now widely recognized as the father of public access television, joined Red Burns, a Canadian documentary filmmaker, to found the Alternate Media Center at New York University. The goal of the Alternate Media Center was to "ensure that new communication technology served the public interest."[14] The Center, located above a movie theatre on Bleecker Street in Greenwich Village, became the hub of the public access television movement in the United States, formulating policy, acting as a clearinghouse for information, and producing public access cable television programming.[15]

One of the first productions of the Alternate Media Center was impromptu and unconventional. As Stoney related in a 1984 interview with Marita Sturken for *Afterimage*: "We wanted to see if people would respond to a different kind of television, so instead of trying to make our stuff look like conventional programming, we just had video crews go [to Washington Heights] and say 'Hey man, what's happening?' and record their response. It was all very laid back. . . . We put the unedited tapes directly on cable as well as having community playbacks."[16] Because so few people had cable service in the early 1970s in New York City, Stoney and Burns would set up viewings in vacant storefronts, community centers, apartment lobbies, and even in the back of Stoney's station wagon so people could watch the programs.

In another instance, after a news article appeared in the *New York Times* about blacks and Hispanics fighting on the street, a member of the Center's staff took a camera to the site and asked people on the street what had happened. Stoney described the video:

One man starts talking, telling what he knows, and people gather around. The next person takes the microphone and the next. Then a wonderful crazy guy starts spinning a big tale and everybody else corrects him. Finally, a young guy from the Catholic school nearby tells them what really happened. When the tape is through you have a feeling, not that you have learned exactly what happened the night before, but that you have learned so much about the dynamics of this neighborhood, that you know it's a neighborhood worth keeping. I think the tape ran as two unedited half hours and we repeated it every day for a week. We found that people often watched it two or three times.[17]

Other Alternate Media Center efforts included organizing public access television efforts in four different locations throughout the United States, implementing an internship program, and helping to found the National Federation of Local Cable Programmers. The organizing effort was implemented in Reading, Pennsylvania; Orlando, Florida; DeKalb, Illinois; and Bakersfield, California. In each instance, the cable company funded the undertaking, which included starting a public access television center, operating it for three to six months, training a local person to take over at the end of the trial period, and then monitoring and advising them after the national staff person returned to New York.

A grant from the National Endowment for the Arts and matching funds from local cable companies helped implement an internship program. Initially, the interns would spend a few weeks with Stoney and Burns at the Alternate Media Center and then would return to their home communities to start public access television there. The interns would return for a week during the middle of the year and then again at the end of their first year to help train the next group of interns. In this way, the Alternate Media Center was able to facilitate the public access television movement in many communities across the country.

With the help and interest of about fifty people nationwide, many of them former interns of Stoney and Burns, the National Federation of Local Cable Programmers was founded in 1976 to act as a clearinghouse for information and advocate for public access television on a national level. In 1978, the NFLCP attracted two hundred fifty people to its annual meeting in Madison, Wisconsin. Just six years later, attendance was up to six hundred attendees at the national conference in Portland, Oregon.[18]

OTHER EARLY PROGRAMMING EFFORTS

But even before Stoney came to New York and before the Alternate Media Center was created, there was a public access television anomaly: DCTV. The franchise for cable service in Dale City, Virginia was held by Cable TV, Inc., and in 1968 this local cable operator provided the first cable channel for community use in the United States. The public access channel, Dale City Television (DCTV), was administered by the Jaycees (Junior Chamber of Commerce) and used two cameras and a one-inch videotape recorder. The DCTV experiment ended in early 1970 primarily because of poor funding and inadequate equipment.[19]

In that same year, two twenty-year, noncompetitive cable franchises were awarded in the borough of Manhattan, one to Sterling Information Services and one to Teleprompter Corporation (now Group W Cable). Initially, the franchise agreements referred only to leased access (cablecast time that is sold at low cost), but during last-minute negotiations it was agreed that two public access channels would be made available free of charge. Teleprompter immediately agreed to provide a studio with one camera, a playback deck, and a director, also free of charge. Sterling also eventually agreed to provide public access television, but generally just scheduled and transmitted completed programming that was delivered to its office. There were also two channels reserved for governmental access.[20]

A year after the beginning of public access television in New York, Teleprompter opened a video access storefront studio in Harlem. So that more people could view the programs that were produced, playbacks were set up in people's homes, in barber shops, and at the Alternate Media Center. By the end of 1971, these two public access channels were cablecasting five to six hours a day.[21]

Once the delivery mechanism for public access television was secured, a dual challenge remained. One was to develop and create programming. The other was to get people to watch. Audiences were limited in 1971 and 1972 because few

people had cable. This meant that access proponents had to undertake a co
hensive marketing campaign that would get the word out about the new public
access television programs, while simultaneously setting up viewings in public
places for the large number of people not yet connected to cable. A prime mover
toward this end was Theodora Sklover, a communications specialist and educator.
As she stated then, "Our biggest problem lies in informing the public that they
can go on television. . . . People are used to thinking of TV as something someone else does, not something they do."[22] Sklover established Open Channel to
produce public access television programming. She saw immediately that outreach and funding were crucial, and she was successful in attracting money from
several foundations. Eventually, she amassed over two hundred television and
film producers, directors, writers, camera operators, and audio and lighting tech-
nicians who would volunteer to help produce public access television programming for community groups.

Open Channel and the Alternate Media Center were not the only groups trying to help people produce programming for public access television in
Manhattan in the early 1970s. Other roots of public access television could be
found in the radical video collectives of the late 1960s and early 1970s. Groups
such as Raindance, Videofreex, People's Communication Network, Video Free
America, Ant Farm, Global Village, the May Day Collective, and People's Video
Theatre were trying to unite the underground press with the new communication
technologies. Michael Shamberg, one of the major proponents of what came to
be called "guerrilla television" and author of a book by the same name, became
a public access television proponent and worked to promote public access channels on cable systems.[23]

THE FCC'S ROLE IN PUBLIC ACCESS TELEVISION

In 1972, Stoney and Burns assisted Federal Communications Commission
member Nicholas Johnson in creating federal access channel requirements that
were reported in the FCC's Cable Television Report and Order. Prior to this ruling, at hearings held by the FCC, public access television had been listed as the
most popular service among potential cable subscribers. This report established
at least four important policies. First, it asserted the FCC's right to regulate
cable television. Second, it gave local governments freedom to negotiate franchise agreements with cable companies. Third, it protected broadcast stations in
the top fifty markets by requiring local cable companies to carry all local broadcast stations within their geographic area (the "must-carry" rules). Fourth, and
most important to this discussion, it required all cable systems with thirty-five
hundred or more subscribers to set aside three noncommercial "access" channels: public (free indefinitely), and educational and governmental (free for at
least five years). Public access television was receiving the kind of attention
and nurture needed for strong growth—and that is just what happened during
the next decade.[24]

THE GROWTH OF PUBLIC ACCESS TELEVISION
WITH CABLE

Interestingly, another early advocate of public access television was the cable industry itself. During this time, as the industry laid cable in hundreds of municipalities, the networks were beginning to feel threatened. Accordingly, they adopted a hard-line competitive stance toward cable operators, an adversarial attitude that persists in many communities to this day. This, in turn, motivated the cable industry to defend its newly won turf. They seized upon public access television as a service that had public relations appeal and could help them to portray their industry as more responsive to local concerns than the networks. To demonstrate its capacity to provide an important public service, the cable industry promoted public access television to show it was a "socially responsible medium." This commitment to public access television helped the cable industry differentiate itself from the network cartel and to legitimate it in the public mind.[25]

Public access television now had the secure backing of the FCC and had established viable, high-profile operations in New York and other major cities. This solid foundation, coupled with the advent of even smaller and easier-to-use video equipment, led to increased interest and activity in public access television. Another boost was the growth of the National Federation of Local Cable Programmers (renamed the Alliance for Community Media in 1992). The NFLCP (now ACM) provides information, assists community producers, holds conferences, serves as a lobbying arm, and produces the journal *Community Media Review* (formerly *Community Television Review*). The federation and the journal were renamed in 1992 to reflect a broader range of community media interests including desktop publishing, low-power radio and television, and the "information highway."[26]

Around the country, cities were negotiating cable contracts: Boston, Pittsburgh, Philadelphia, Los Angeles, and Cincinnati, among others. In some cases, small cities or suburbs would franchise jointly in order to attract more favorable bids and to obtain better service. In one case, six cities south of Dayton, Ohio, came together to form the Miami Valley Cable Council to "regulate cable, and pool their franchise fees to pay for regulatory costs and to support cable access." Many medium-to-small-sized cities and towns did not get cable until the late 1970s or early 1980s.[27]

This period of steady growth was not without its setbacks. The most significant threat came from the Supreme Court. In a 1979 case, *FCC v. Midwest Video*, the Court invalidated the FCC's public, educational, and governmental (PEG) access requirements, stating that the FCC had overstepped its authority. The Court went on to say that Congress *did* have the authority to require PEG access, if it chose to exercise it. This ruling created a great deal of uncertainty that would not be cleared up until the passage of the Cable Communications Act in 1984.

But the growth of public access television was assured simply because the growth of the cable industry itself had created a buyer's market. The competition between cable companies for local franchises was often intense. Opportunistic and forward-thinking communities were able to demand access facilities in exchange for awarding their franchises to certain cable operators. In an extreme case, Dallas–Fort Worth was able to get twenty-four access channels.[28]

In some areas progress was slower. Although the cable franchise for Brooklyn, New York was awarded in 1983, the borough was not wired until 1987. Additional bureaucratic delays resulted from snags in negotiations between the city and the cable companies involved, and it was not until the end of 1990 that public access television was implemented in the city. At that time, Brooklyn Public Access Corporation was formed to administer the four public access channels. Currently, programming airs on three channels and a fourth channel airs a continuous bulletin board.[29]

CONTINUED GROWTH

Throughout the 1980s, public access television activity continued to take root throughout the country: Somerville (Massachusetts) Community TV, Goddard's Community Media Center, Brattleboro (Vermont) Community Television, and Austin Community Access Center in Austin, Texas are a few of the local operations that developed and expanded during this period. And people using public access television began to see themselves and the world in a different way. As Lauren-Glenn Davitian, founder and coordinator of Chittenden Community Television and Vermont Television Network, the state's first and largest public affairs cable access network, explained:

Public access was more than free speech—it was an instrument of local animation and change. The earliest projects, like many produced today, rallied support around pressing local issues: the missing stop sign at a busy Newark intersection, the concerns of Reading, Ohio's elderly, [and] the rights of Chinese tenants on New York's lower East Side.[30]

Public access television was taking root in communities around the country. Public access television activists in large cities as well as in smaller, progressive ones were beginning to mobilize and ask for public access television.

One of the best and longest running examples of public access television programming began in Austin, Texas in 1978. "Alternative Views" started as a long-format interview show that focused on issues not usually covered by the mainstream media. Over the years, the show evolved and incorporated documentary films, slide shows, and raw video footage. People interviewed on the show include Austinite Ray Reece on corporate control and suppression of solar energy; John Stockwell on how he was recruited into the CIA at the University of Texas at Austin and why he thought the CIA should be shut down; American

Atheist founder Madalyn Murray O'Hair; Stokeley Carmichael (now Kwame Ture) on black power; Nobel Prize winner George Wald; Ramsey Clark, former United States Attorney General; and Helen Caldicott, antinuclear activist. As Douglas Kellner writes in his book *Television and the Crisis of Democracy*:

Various feminists, gays, union activists, and representatives of local progressive groups have appeared as guests on our show. We have also carried . . . in-depth interviews with officials from the Soviet Union and Nicaragua, Allende's former government in Chile, members of the democratic front in El Salvador, and participants in other Third World revolutionary movements. . . . We have also received raw video footage of the bombing of Lebanon and the aftermath of the massacres at Sabra and Shatilla, of the assassinations of five communist labor organizers by the Ku Klux Klan in Greensboro, NC, of daily life in the liberated zones of El Salvador, and of counterrevolutionary activity in Nicaragua.[31]

Because of its embodiment of most of the goals of public access television, "Alternative Views" is often regarded as a model of public access television programming. By 1996 it was just one of thousands of programs being aired on local public access stations nationwide. There were over four thousand PEG systems in operation by that time.[32]

CONTROVERSIAL PROGRAMMING

Given cameras, air time, and few restrictions, it was inevitable that public access television producers would test the limits of socially acceptable television programming. In the 1970s and 1980s, controversial shows on public access television caused consternation in various communities. In 1974, the first cablecast on a new system in Somerville, Massachusetts, "Video Shorts," produced by the Somerville Media Action Project, included one segment of a dog urinating on a local fire hydrant and another of a young marine using off-color language as he gets a haircut in preparation for his induction. "Midnight Blue" and "Ugly George," two R-rated shows that had been airing for several years in New York City, not only raised the hackles of local viewers but confirmed the opinion of many in the heartland that Manhattan was a den of iniquity. A little further north, several students from the State University of New York produced a show called "Aunt Ketty" in New Rochelle, New York, in which the host portrayed a transvestite who is raped by a floor lamp and, in a graphic birth scene, gives birth to a table lamp. Many viewers found this spectacle neither amusing nor edifying.[33]

All across the country, in hundreds of documented and undocumented instances, local producers were testing local tolerance for unpopular or potentially offensive programming. In Cincinnati, a neo-Nazi group used the public access television community bulletin board to get out their recruitment message. This kind of use tested local support for public access television. In several instances, communities tried to ban the programming in question.

In 1989, Kansas City closed its public access channel to keep the Ku Klux Klan from airing its program "Race and Reason." This show, produced by former California KKK Grand Dragon Tom Metzger, first aired in Pocatello, Idaho, in 1985. Kansas City was sued by the KKK for denial of its First Amendment rights of free speech, and the court ruled in favor of the Klan. Kansas City had to reinstate its public access channel and allow cablecast of the program.[34]

In more recent instances, Los Angeles Mayor Richard Riordan vetoed a $375,000 payment to the public access organization because he did not like some of the programming, even though he was advised that the city council could not control content on access channels.[35] And when the local media focused on public access programming in the Portland, Oregon area that featured a man who undressed on the air, local public access supporters placed advertisements in the *Oregonian*, Portland's main newspaper, proclaiming the importance of public access. The tag line for the ads was "Cable Access: It's Not Just One Naked Guy."[36]

Although the Kansas City reaction was the most extreme, several other incidents of "hate groups" using public access television to spread their messages cropped up in the 1980s. Most communities found that, after the initial shock of such offensive or controversial messages (one message on a community bulletin board said "Join the Nazis and smash Red, Jew, and Black Power"), the best way to allay fears and minimize hostility was to air other programs that put forth more constructive and socially acceptable points of view. The Anti-Defamation League recruited documentarist Matt Barr to create the video "Crimes of Hate" as a direct rebuttal to "Race and Reason," and made the tape and a discussion guide available to anyone. Or, as the former director of the Cincinnati Cable Access Corporation put it, and as many public access advocates agree, "the answer to bad speech is more speech."[37]

PUBLIC ACCESS TELEVISION REGULATIONS

In the early 1980s, two forces combined to put pressure on Congress to clarify the role of the cable industry in general, and of public access television in particular. First, the cable industry, faced with slowing growth, was calling for less federal regulation. Second, it had become increasingly clear that Congress needed to settle the question of whether cable operators would be obligated to provide public access television services or whether it would remain voluntary, a matter to be settled in negotiation between cable companies and the local municipalities that awarded cable franchises. In response, Congress formulated the Cable Communications Policy Act of 1984. This law provided long-overdue amendments to the Communications Act of 1934. One of the six purposes of the 1984 Cable Act was to "assure that cable communications provide and are encouraged to provide the widest possible diversity of information sources and service to the public." The act clearly gave local governmental entities the authority to require cable operators to provide channels for public access television (along with educational and governmental access).[38]

The Cable Communications Policy Act of 1984 and the Cable Television Consumer Protection and Competition Act of 1992 (both of which amended the 1934 Communications Act) contained language that allowed franchisers to require PEG access as part of their negotiated agreements. Significantly, the acts do not require the cable operators to provide public access television, but allow the franchisers, usually local governments, to require public access television as part of their franchise agreements. If the franchisers did not require it, the cable operators would not have to provide it. This regulation effectively placed the onus on the citizenry. If they wanted public access television, they would have to organize and lobby local governmental officials during the franchise negotiations to demand access services. This served to further legitimate negotiations for public access television, but it did not make it easy. As late as September 1998, Orlando, Florida did not have public access television, although the city does have government access television. The local group, Community Media Associates, has been lobbying for public access, but it has been an uphill battle.[39]

The 1992 Act, passed by Congress over President Bush's veto, added several provisions related to PEG access while leaving intact PEG provisions contained in the 1984 Cable Act. One provision requires PEG access channels to be carried on the basic tier (Channels 2 to 13), and another made cable operators responsible for the content of programs aired on the public access television channels carried on their system. The 1984 Cable Act had given cable operators immunity from state law if they transmitted obscenity over PEG and leased access. The 1992 Cable Act took away this immunity. Cable operators could now be held responsible for any obscene programming on PEG access channels, and they could be criminally charged. (The United States Supreme Court eventually overruled this part of the act.)[40]

Several court cases challenged public access television during the 1980s and early 1990s, but in each case the underlying principles of public access television were upheld.[41] (See Chapter 2 for detailed review of public access television regulations and court cases.)

By the early 1990s public access television was flourishing in many communities across the country. The vision was still intact, if somewhat unfocused. Along the way, the idea of public access television came to be seen as a First Amendment issue instead of one of community discourse, social change, and empowerment. Or, as Robert H. Devine, Communications Department Chair at Antioch College, has written: "Those who do make the connection between access and the First Amendment often focus on those dimensions dealing with autonomy of private expression without much regard for the other thread of the First Amendment—the utilitarian notion of forming public opinion through public discourse."[42]

Of course, public access television in any form would not exist at all if not for the support of the FCC, Congress, and the courts. The next chapter focuses on the regulations and court cases that have helped shape public access television over the past thirty years.

NOTES

1. Douglas Kellner, *Television and the Crisis of Democracy* (Boulder, CO: Westview, 1990), 201–2; and Ralph Engelman, *Public Radio and Television in America: A Political History* (Thousand Oaks, CA: Sage Publications, 1996), 145–65.

2. Quoted in Engelman, *Public Radio and Television in America*, 154.

3. William Safire, written for a speech given by Vice President Spiro Agnew in San Diego, September 11, 1970, cited in William Safire, *Safire's Political Dictionary* (New York: Random House, 1978), 444–45.

4. Engelman, *Public Radio and Television in America*, 167–68.

5. Ralph Engelman, "The Origins of Public Access Cable Television 1966–1972," *Journalism Monographs* 123 (October 1990): 4, 1; Eric Barnouw, *Tube of Plenty: The Evolution of American Television* (New York: Oxford University Press, 1977), 436; Alex McNeil, *Total Television: A Comprehensive Guide to Programming from 1948 to the Present* (New York: Penguin, 1984), 474.

6. Engelman, "The Origins of Public Access Cable Television," 4; and Engelman, *Public Radio and Television in America*, 169.

7. Engelman, *Public Radio and Television in America*, 166; Gilbert Gillespie, *Public Access Cable Television in the United States and Canada* (New York: Praeger, 1975), 10, 21; John D. Hollinrake, Jr., "Cable Television: Public Access and the First Amendment," *Communications and the Law* 9, no. 1 (February 1987): 40.

8. Quoted in Marita Sturken, "An Interview with George Stoney," *Afterimage* (January 1984): 7; Engelman, "The Origins of Public Access Cable Television," 6–7; Gillespie, 26–29.

9. Engelman, "The Origins of Public Access Cable Television," 12; A. William Bluem, *Documentary in American Television* (New York: Hastings House, 1979), 46; Gillespie, 32–33.

10. Engelman, *Public Radio and Television in America*, 226.

11. Ibid.

12. Sturken, 7; Engelman, "The Origins of Public Access Cable Television," 14–15; Gillespie, 34–35.

13. Engelman, "The Origins of Public Access Cable Television," 18.

14. Ibid., 24.

15. Engelman, *Public Radio and Television in America*, 235.

16. Quoted in Sturken, 9.

17. Ibid., 9.

18. Ibid., 10.

19. Linda K. Fuller, *Community Television in the United States: A Sourcebook on Public, Educational, and Governmental Access*, (Westport, CT: Greenwood Press, 1994): 145.

20. Quoted in Engelman, "The Origins of Public Access Cable Television," 33.

21. Engelman, "The Origins of Public Access Cable Television," 20; Kirsten Beck, *Cultivating the Wasteland: Can Cable Put the Vision back in Television?* (New York: American Council for the Arts, 1983), 113–14. See also Nicholas Johnson and Gary G. Gerlach, "The Coming Fight for Public Access," *Yale Review of Law and Social Action* 2

(1972): 220–22; Barry T. Janes, "History and Structure of Public Access Television," *Journal of Film and Video* 39 (Summer 1987): 14; Engelman, *Public Radio and Television in America*, 39; Gillespie, 4–5; Lauren Glenn-Davitian, "Building the Empire: Access as Community Animation," *Journal of Film and Video* 39 (Summer 1987): 35; and Ross Corson, "Cable's Missed Connection: A Revolution that Won't Be Televised," in *American Mass Media: Industries and Issues*, ed. Robert Atwan, et al., (New York: Random House, 1986), 381.

22. Gillespie, 48; Engelman, "The Origins of Public Access Cable Television," 33–34; Sturken, 9.

23. Janes, 15–16; Gillespie, 35–36; Engelman, "The Origins of Public Access Cable Television," 32–33; Sturken, 8. See also Monroe E. Price and John Wicklein, *Cable Television: A Guide for Citizen Action* (Philadelphia: Pilgrim Press, 1972), 67–69.

24. Janes, 17, and Davitian, 36.

25. Gillespie, 39–40; Engelman, "The Origins of Public Access Cable Television," 27.

26. Janes, 18; Jean Rice, "The Communications Pipeline," *Public Management* (June 1980): 3. See also Sue Miller Buske, "Improving Local Community Access Programming," *Public Management* 62, no. 5 (June 1980): 12; Thelma Vickroy, "Live from Norwalk: How One City Saved Community Programming," *Journal of Film and Video* 39 (Summer 1987): 24.

27. Davitian, 36; Janes, 17–19; Sturken, 8–9; and Corson, 380.

28. Davitian, 36.

29. Esther Iverem, "Public Access Programs Scheduled for Brooklyn," *Newsday* (4 July 1990): 29.

30. Ibid.

31. Kellner, 209–10. See also Engelman, *Public Radio and Television in America*, 245–55. Kellner, one of the founders of "Alternative Views," is a professor of philosophy at the University of Texas at Austin and is the author of *Herbert Marcuse and the Crisis of Marxism*, *Jean Baudrillard*, and *Critical Theory, Marxism, and Modernity*, among others.

32. Brett Briller, "Accent on Access Television," *Television Quarterly* 28, no. 2 (Spring 1996): 51.

33. Janes, 14–23.

34. Mark D. Harmon, "Hate Groups and Cable Public Access," *Journal of Mass Media Ethics* 6, no. 3 (1991): 149, 153.

35. John M. Higgins, "L.A. Mayor Rejects Public Access Funding," *Broadcasting and Cable* 128, no. 36 (31 August 1998): 47.

36. David Raths, "Building Community," *Business Journal* 13 (14 June 1996): 12.

37. Ibid., 149–50.

38. *Cable Communications Policy Act of 1984, U.S. Code*, vol. 47, sec. 531 (1984).

39. *Cable Communications Policy Act of 1984, U.S. Code*, vol. 47, sec. 611 (1984); *Cable Television Consumer Protection and Competition Act of 1992, U.S. Code*, vol. 47, sec. 531–59 (1992); and Paul Dillon, "Activist Urges County to Rethink Public-Access TV," *Orlando Business Journal* 15 (28 August–3 September 1998): 3, 62.

40. James N. Horwood, "Public, Educational, and Governmental Access on Cable Television: A Model to Assure Reasonable Access to the Information Superhighway for All People in Fulfillment of the First Amendment Guarantee of Free Speech," *Seton Hall Law Review* 25 (1995): 1415; Nicholas P. Miller and Joseph Van Eaton, "A Review of Developments in Cases Defining the Scope of the First Amendment Rights of Cable Television Operators," *Cable Television Law* 2 (1993): 298.

41. *Preferred Communications v. City of Los Angeles*, 754 F.2d 1396 (9th Cir. 1985); *Berkshire Cablevision v. Burke*, 659 F.Supp. 580 (W.D. Pa. 1987); *Erie Telecommunications v. City of Erie*, 723 F.Supp. 1347 (W.D. Mo. 1989); and *Missouri Knights of the Ku Klux Klan v. City of Kansas City, Missouri*, 723 F.Supp. 1347 (W.D. Mo. 1989).

42. Robert H. Devine, "Video, Access and Agency." (Paper presented at the annual convention of the National Federation of Local Cable Programmers, Saint Paul, Minnesota, 17 July 1992), 1.

2

Making Sense of Public Access Regulations

The history of cable public access television regulations cannot be reviewed adequately without tracing some of the history of cable regulations in general. There is a hierarchy to cable regulations, with one level building upon another. Initially, this chapter will focus on the full range of cable law, with a greater focus on public access television as the regulations and court cases begin to deal with the particular legal issues that came to the fore as public access television grew.

THE FCC ASSERTS AUTHORITY TO REGULATE CABLE TELEVISION

The beginning of cable regulation dates to 1965, when the Federal Communications Commission issued a *First Report and Order* maintaining the FCC's authority to regulate cable television (CATV; then called community antenna television): "We have determined as an initial matter that the Communications Act [of 1934] vests in this agency appropriate rulemaking authority over all CATV systems, including those which do not use microwave relay service (the so-called 'off-the-air' systems)."[1] This was the first time the FCC had asserted its jurisdiction over the burgeoning cable television business.

In 1968, the United States Supreme Court heard a case unrelated to cable television that would delineate the circumstances under which the government could regulate speech. The case was *United States v. O'Brien*, and the test, which came to be known as the *O'Brien* test, said: "[A] government regulation is sufficiently justified if it is within the constitutional power of the Government; if it furthers an important or substantial governmental interest; if the government interest is unrelated to the suppression of free speech; and if the incidental restriction on alleged First Amendment freedoms is no greater than is essential to the further-ance of that interest."[2] Since public access television would become a free speech forum, the *O'Brien* test would become important to future public access televi-sion regulation.

Another challenge to the FCC's jurisdiction came before the United States Supreme Court in 1968 in *United States v. Southwestern Cable Co.* Once again the Court ruled that the FCC had jurisdiction over cable television: "We therefore hold that the Commission's authority over 'all interstate . . . communication by wire or radio' permits the regulation of CATV systems. . . . The Commission may, for these purposes, issue 'such rules and regulations and prescribe such restric-tions and conditions, not inconsistent with law,' *as public convenience, interest, or necessity requires.*"[3]

A year later, the Supreme Court issued another ruling that would affect future cases involving public access television. In *Red Lion Broadcasting Co. v. FCC*, the Court held that

Because of the scarcity of radio frequencies, the Government is permitted to put restraints on licensees in favor of others whose views should be expressed on the unique medium. But the people as a whole retain their interest in free speech by radio and their collective right to have the medium function consistently with the ends and purposes of the First Amendment. It is the *right of the viewers and listeners*, not the right of the broadcasters, which is paramount.[4]

This case, along with *O'Brien*, would be referred to often in future cases con-cerning public access television. But the regulatory waters in this area remained calm for over twenty years, primarily due to the limited availability of cable tele-vision. As cable proliferated in the 1970s and 1980s, however, points of legal con-tention inevitably came to the fore.

PROMISE OF CABLE PUBLIC ACCESS TELEVISION

The FCC began testing the public access television waters when it issued a *Notice of Proposed Rulemaking* and *Notice of Inquiry* in December 1968. The *Notice* said that "the potential contribution of CATV in this respect, both as a means of providing a local outlet to communities which have no television broadcast out-let of their own and as a means of enhancing diversity in communities which do have broadcast outlets . . . offers sufficient promise to be encouraged."[5] This *Notice* solicited comments from all interested parties. In a followup *Notice of Proposed Rulemaking* in July 1970, the Commission stated:

The structure and operation of our system of radio and television broadcasting affects, among other things, the sense of "community" of those within the signal area of the sta-tions involved. Recently, governmental programs have been directed toward increasing cit-izen involvement in community affairs. *Cable television has the potential to be a vehicle for much needed community expression.* To strengthen the sense of community and allow greater communication, *cable systems should supply a separate channel*, available on a when-desired basis, for each distinct community within its franchised area. It will also be necessary that each community possess the capability for production of material to be cable cast over its channel.[6]

Then FCC Commissioner Nicholas Johnson wrote a concurring statement in support of public access television that said:

The Federal Communications Commission must be responsible for the human and socio-logical implications of its decisions, as well as the economic, technological, and political consequences. *The structure and operation of our country's communications system—*especially the mass media—*affect*, among many other things, *the sense of "community" of those who both benefit from and are used by the system.*

Those who study and write about the trends in our society report a growing sense of alienation, loneliness, emptiness, despair, and hostility among the central city residents in the larger urban areas. Many believe that these trends are, at least in part, exacerbated by the existence of television and radio stations which have been authorized by the FCC to serve audiences of millions, rather than neighborhoods and small urban areas. . . .

Cable systems have the potential to remedy this situation. With unlimited channel capacity, programming aimed at small communities can be cablecast and *origination by members of the local neighborhood community are possible*. But none of this is possible without the installation of systems capable of providing channel capacity to anyone at any-time upon demand. . . . Because of this, perhaps our *most important decision* today is the proposal that all new systems be of a specified minimum size, that they have the capabil-ity of two-way switching, and that *they provide community channels and community cen-ters for programming those channels*.[7]

The FCC seemed to be saying that by having a local media outlet not con-trolled by others, public access television could help people feel less alienated from and more connected to one another in their neighborhoods and communi-ties. This statement, like so many others of the early FCC rules and regulations, placed a high value on local expression and diversity.

In August 1971, FCC regulations regarding cable public access television stated that "certain basic goals of the Communications Act [could] be fur-thered by cable's advent—the opening up of new outlets for local program-ming, the promotion of added diversity in television programming, the advancement of educational and instructional television, and the increased information services of local governments."[8] The FCC would require "one free, dedicated, non-commercial, public access channel available at all times on a non-discriminatory basis . . . one channel set aside for educational use and one channel for state and local government use on a developmental basis."[9] Additionally, no advertising, lotteries, or obscene or indecent material would be allowed on the channels. These were considered to be interim rules and were created for two stated purposes: "(1) to allow maximum experimentation and (2) to prevent, particularly during this critical early period and probably at all times, one entity sitting astride all this channel capacity and deciding which programming should or should not enter subscriber homes."[10] The

Commission went on to say, "We recognize that open access carries with it certain risks. But some amount of risk is inherent in a democracy committed to fostering 'uninhibited, robust, and wide-open' debate on public issues."[11]

These public access television requirements were challenged in a case decided by the U.S. Supreme Court in June 1972. In *United States v. Midwest Video Corp.* (*Midwest Video I*), the Court affirmed the FCC's right to regulate cable television. The majority of the justices held that "the regulatory authority asserted by the Commission in 1966 and generally sustained by this Court in *Southwestern* was authority to regulate CATV with a view not merely to protect but to promote the objectives for which the Commission had been assigned jurisdiction over broadcasting."[12] The Court went on to say that "The Commission is not attempting to compel wire service where there has been no commitment to undertake it. CATV operators to whom the cablecasting rule applies have voluntarily engaged themselves in providing that service, and the Commission seeks only to ensure that it satisfactorily meets community needs within the context of their understanding. For these reasons we conclude that the program-origination rule is within the Commission's authority recognized in *Southwestern*."[13]

The FCC issued formal regulations regarding public access television later that year in its *Cable Television Report and Order*:

[I]t is therefore appropriate that the fundamental goals of a national communications structure be furthered by cable—the opening of new outlets for local expression, the promotion of diversity in television programming, the advancement of educational and instructional television, and the increased informational services of local governments. . . .

[W]e believe there is increasing need for channels for community expression, and the steps we are taking are designed to serve that need. The public access channel will offer a practical opportunity to participate in community dialogue through a mass medium. A system operator located in a major television market will be obliged to provide only use of the channel without charge, but production costs (aside from live studio presentations not exceeding five minutes in length) may be charged to users.[14]

The provisions also required channels for educational and governmental purposes. Local regulation of the public access channel was prohibited, and access to the channel was to be nondiscriminatory and on a first-come, first-serve basis. Advertising, lottery information, and obscene or indecent material was prohibited.[15]

Another U.S. Supreme Court case, *Miami Herald Publishing Co. v. Tornillo*, would come to haunt public access television advocates because it seemed to set a "no access" precedent. In this 1974 case, the Court ruled that government-required public access to a newspaper violates the First Amendment's guarantee of a free press:

Even if a newspaper would face no additional costs to comply with a compulsory access law and would not be forced to forgo publication of news or opinion by the inclusion of a reply, the Florida statute fails to clear the barriers of the First Amendment because of its intrusion into the function of editors. A newspaper is more than a passive receptacle or conduit for news, comment, and advertising. The choice of material to go into a newspaper, and the decisions made as to limitations on the size and content of the paper, and the treatment of public issues and public officials—whether fair or unfair—constitute the exercise of editorial control and judgment. It has yet to be demonstrated how government regulation of this crucial process can be exercised consistent with First Amendment guarantees of a free press as they have evolved to this time.[16]

If the *Tornillo* case had been applied to cable companies as well as newspapers, public access would not have been allowed. However, the Court (and the FCC) have always seen and treated broadcasting and cable as different from one another and from the press.

The court continued to delineate a difference between the press, broadcasting, and cable in *American Civil Liberties Union v. FCC*. In a 1975 case, the Ninth Circuit Court of Appeals held that the FCC could regulate cable operators as common carriers. The Court of Appeals equated cable with telephone companies—relayers of information—without First Amendment rights.[17] But later that year in a case unrelated to public access television, the United States Supreme Court stated:

[T]he concept that government may restrict the speech of some elements of our society in order to enhance the relative voice of others is wholly foreign to the First Amendment, which was designed "to secure the widest possible dissemination of information from diverse and antagonistic sources," and "to assure unfettered interchange of ideas for the bringing about of political and social changes desired by the people." . . . The First Amendment's protection against governmental abridgment of free expression cannot properly be made to depend on a person's financial ability to engage in public discussion.[18]

This decision, which grew out of Congress' attempt to restrict campaign spending by the wealthy, caused some concern among public access supporters and advocates. Future rulings, however, would counter this logic by allowing minimal restriction of cable operators' speech in order to promote more speech via public access television. As long as the courts treated cable as a common carrier or as a limited resource, public access television would be unaffected.

THE SUPREME COURT INVALIDATES PUBLIC ACCESS TELEVISION REQUIREMENTS

That same year the FCC revised its 1972 public, education, and governmental (PEG) access requirements; the commissioners commented that

There is, we believe, a definite societal good in keeping these channels of communication. While the overall impact that use of these channels can have may have been exaggerated in the past, nevertheless we believe they can, if properly used, result in the opening of new outlets for local expression, aid in the promotion of diversity in television programming, act in some measure to restore a sense of community to cable subscribers and a sense of openness and participation to the video medium, aid in the functioning of democratic institutions, and improve the informational and educational communications resources of cable television communities.

On the other hand, these public benefits must be carefully weighed against the costs the requirements impose. . . . Thus, abstract notions of public good must be carefully tested as to their cost and practical, realistic impact.[19]

The changes made to the public access television regulations were to apply the rules to all systems with thirty-five hundred or more subscribers, whether they were in a major market or not, and to apply the rules to cable systems rather than to communities. The amended rules also required four access channels only if there was a demand for their use and only in those systems with sufficient capacity.

The commissioners also addressed some of the concerns that had been raised about their jurisdiction over cable and the obligation of cable operators to provide public access. Quoting the U.S. Supreme Court in *Midwest Video I*, the commissioners reiterated their intention "to 'promote the objectives for which [we] have been assigned jurisdiction over broadcasting.' Among those *objectives recognized by the Court are increasing the number of outlets for local self-expression and augmenting the diversity of programs and types of services available to the public*. The Supreme Court upheld the agency's determination that the program-origination rule would serve those objectives. It is equally plain that channel capacity and *access requirements will promote those objectives.*"[20]

Throughout the 1960s and into the 1970s a consistent legal stumbling block was the lack of a clear definition of exactly what constitutes a cable system. Quoting its own *Cable Television Report and Order*, however, the FCC maintained a middle-of-the-road position: "[C]able is a hybrid that requires identification and regulation as a separate force in communications."[21] Defining cable would continue to vex the courts for the next two decades.

Three cases only marginally related to public access television were heard within the next two years, all of which served to reaffirm the FCC's jurisdiction over cable. The first two were *National Association of Regulating Utility Commissioners v. Federal Communications Commission*[22] (dealing with diversity and leased access) and *Home Box Office, Inc. v. Federal Communications Commission* (the first FCC case to apply the *O'Brien* test).[23] In the third case, *Brookhaven Cable TV, Inc. v. Kelly*, which would become important in later cases, the Court of Appeals interpreted the decision of the U.S. Supreme Court rulings: "[I]t approved the FCC's mandatory cable origination goals as 'reasonably ancillary' to 'the achievement of *long-established broadcasting goals in the field of television broadcasting by increasing the number of outlets for community self-expression* and augmenting the public's choice of programs and type of service.' It follows that the FCC may regulate cable TV if its regulation will further a goal which it is entitled to pursue in the broadcast arena."[24] These three cases affirmed the FCC's role in the regulation of cable television and seemed to affirm the concept of public access television. The courts veered from this path later that year, however.

In a sharp departure from past cases that seemed to condone and even approve of the FCC's public access television requirements, the U.S. Supreme Court invalidated the PEG access regulations in *Federal Communications Commission v. Midwest Video Corp.* (hereinafter *Midwest Video II*) in 1979. The crux was that the rules imposed common-carrier status on cable operators and thereby deprived them of editorial control of programming. Building on the argument first expressed in Justice Douglas' dissent in 1972 in *United States v. Midwest Video Corporation (Midwest Video I)*,[25] the Court concluded:

In light of the hesitancy with which Congress approached the access issue in the broadcast area, and in view of its outright rejection of a broad right of public access on a common-carrier basis, this Court is constrained to hold that the FCC exceeded the limits of its authority in promulgating its access rules. The FCC may not regulate cable systems as common carriers, just as it may not impose such obligations on television broadcasters. Authority to compel cable operators to provide common carriage of public-originated transmissions must come specifically from Congress.[26]

Justice Stevens' dissent in *Midwest Video II* ended with a discussion of an earlier Court case, *Columbia Broadcasting System, Inc. v. Democratic National Committee*:

We emphasized . . . that "Congress has time and again rejected various legislative attempts that would have mandated a variety of forms of individual access." But we went on to conclude: "That is not to say that Congress' rejection of such proposals must be taken to mean that Congress is opposed to private rights of access under all circumstances. *Rather, the point is that Congress has chosen to leave such questions with the Commission, to which it has given the flexibility to experiment with new ideas as changing conditions require.*"
The Commission here has exercised its "flexibility to experiment" in choosing to replace the mandatory origination rule upheld in *Midwest Video (I)* with what it views as the less onerous local access rules at issue here. I have no reason to doubt its conclusion that these rules, like the mandatory origination rule they replace, do promote the statutory objectives of "increasing the number of outlets for community self-expression and augmenting the public's choice of programs and types of services."[27]

Although this was a dissent, the Court used this rationale to overturn the FCC's public access rule. This same reasoning would eventually be used by Congress to reinstate the requirement that PEG access be provided on cable systems.

Public access television was briefly mentioned in a 1980 case involving cable systems' use of public right-of-ways. The U.S. District Court asked in *Community Communications Company v. City of Boulder*: "[I]s it appropriate for the City administration to say that the acceptability of a cable company rests on its willingness to contribute free services to that government or to such institutions or groups as may be considered to be in need of benefit or reward? Stated bluntly, may the City exact tribute for its favor?"[28] The court did not answer its questions, but noted that they would have to be answered in the future. The issue of PEG access as a quid pro quo for receiving a cable franchise would arise again and would pose legal problems in the future.

OBSCENITY AND INDECENCY ON PUBLIC ACCESS TELEVISION

One perplexing issue that came up earlier rather than later was the issue of obscenity and indecency on public access channels. How would it be controlled? Who was responsible? In *Community Television of Utah v. Roy City*, the U.S. District Court stated:

I emphasize again and again and again public tolerance is not public approval. . . . [I]t should be noted that if I subscribe to a magazine, I need not open its cover. I may pick and choose among the articles. If displeased, I may cancel my subscription. The same is true in subscribing to cable television service. I need not hook up. I need not tune in. I may pick and choose among the programs and I may cancel. . . .

Beyond the line drawn in *Miller*, public bodies must not step—indeed, cannot step—in the control of artistic communication content.[29]

Although this case was not about public access television per se (it concerned regular cable programming), it included an illustrative comparison of cable to broadcast television, which would be used in future cases concerning public access television. (See Table 2.1.) The courts would continue to struggle with exactly what cable was, was not, or was most like, for years to come. The Ku Klux Klan, as cited in Chapter 2, sued Kansas City in 1989 when the city deleted

Table 2.1
Comparison of Cable Television to Broadcast Television

Cable	*Broadcast*
User needs to subscribe.	User need not subscribe.
User holds power to cancel subscriptions.	User holds no power to cancel.
User may complain to cable company.	User may complain to FCC, station, network, or sponsor.
Advertising is limited.	Advertising is extensive.
Transmitted through wires.	Signals transmitted through public airwaves.
User receives signal on private cable.	User appropriates signal from the public airwaves.
User pays a fee.	User does not pay a fee.
User receives preview of coming public press attractions.	User receives daily and weekly listing in commercial guides.
Wires are privately owned.	Airwaves are publicly controlled.

Source: *Community Television of Utah v. Roy City*, 555 F. Supp 1164 (1982), 1167.

its public access channel to keep the KKK from airing its program.[30] The District Court ruled that "[T]he Constitution forbids a state to enforce exclusions from a forum generally open to the public even if it was not required to create the forum in the first place."[31] The court went on to say: "[T]he plaintiffs have an implied right of action under Section 611 of the Cable Act."[32] This thereby gives further credibility to the FCC's access rules contained in the 1984 Cable Act. Also notable is the reference to public access television as a public forum—if public access television is a public forum, then, according to the Supreme Court, "[A]ll parties have a constitutional right of access and the State must demonstrate compelling reasons for restricting access to a single class of speakers, a single viewpoint, or a single subject."[33] Being judged a public forum provided further legitimization for public access television. The Kansas City case sent a clear signal across the country that public access television could withstand not only legal challenges but also the fears that open access to the airwaves were bound to elicit in almost any community.

However, when obscenity and indecency have been at issue, rather than free speech, public access producers have not always fared as well in the courts. In a 1995 Texas case, a three-minute segment of a program entitled "Infosex" was charged with being obscene. The producers of the program maintained that the purpose of the video segment was to encourage safe sex and that it was educational. They further argued that the state had to prove the entire two-hour program was obscene and must use expert testimony to do so. The Texas Court of Appeals for the Third District ruled in *Rees v. State of Texas* that the trial court's finding that the video lacked any redeeming social value was sufficient and that they did not need to provide expert testimony to make their case.[34] The U.S. Supreme Court refused to hear the case and let stand the conviction. This is one example of a community imposing its standards on local public access programming.

SUPREME COURT DEFINES PUBLIC FORUM

In another case that seemed then only peripherally related to public access television, the U.S. Supreme Court delineated two types of public forums: "places which by long tradition or by government fiat have been devoted to assembly and debate [in which] the rights of the State to limit expressive activity are sharply circumscribed . . . [and] public property which the State has opened for use by the public as a place for expressive activity."[35] The Court went on to say: "In a public forum, by definition, all parties have a constitutional right of access and the State must demonstrate compelling reasons for restricting access to a single class of speakers, a single viewpoint, or a single subject."[36] This ruling would come to have significance in a later case when the idea of public access television as a public forum began to gain legitimacy.

In another 1984 case, *Capital Cities Cable v. Crisp*, the Supreme Court once again recognized the FCC's jurisdiction over cable and went on to distinguish the FCC's regulation from state and local regulation. "Over the past 20 years, ρursuant to its delegated authority under the Communications Act [of 1934], the FCC has unambiguously expressed its intent to pre-empt any state or local regulation of this entire array of signals carried by cable television systems."[37] The Court validated the FCC's preemption of state and local laws. Federal law, not state or local law, would govern cable television (and public access television).

To this stage, although real franchises, real policies, and real dollars were at stake, relatively few people were affected by, or interested in, the constitutional issues surrounding public access television. But as this new service became a reality in more cities, the public began to take a greater interest. Gradually, this brought greater pressure to bear on federal legislators and regulators.

CABLE COMMUNICATION'S POLICY ACT OF 1984 AND PUBLIC ACCESS TELEVISION

After considerable discussion and debate over several years, Congress enacted the Cable Communication's Policy Act of 1984 (1984 Cable Act), amending the Communications Act of 1934. One of the six stated purposes of the 1984 Cable Act was to "assure that cable communications provide and are encouraged to provide the widest possible diversity of information sources and service to the public."[38] The act allowed franchisers to require cable operators to provide channel capacity for public access television (along with educational and governmental). It did not require the cable operators to provide public access television; it only allowed the franchisers, usually municipalities, to require public access channels as part of their franchise agreements. Again, if the franchisers did not require public access, the cable operators would not have to provide it. The law supported franchisers, but the responsibility was on the general public to express a demand for public access television.[39]

Also included in the act were rules that required cable operators to transmit over their systems every local over-the-air channel available in their area (known as the must-carry rules). This rule was challenged immediately in the courts. The first case to be decided was *Quincy Cable TV v. Federal Communications Commission* in 1985 in which the United States Court of Appeals ruled that the must-carry rules as they were written in the 1984 Cable Act violated the First Amendment. "We have now concluded and now hold that the must-carry rules are fundamentally at odds with the First Amendment and, as currently drafted, can no longer be permitted to stand."[40]

The court went on to make a comparison between must-carry rules and public access television rules, noting that, "unlike access rules, which serve countervailing First Amendment values by providing a forum for public or governmental authorities, the must-carry rules transfer control to local broadcasters who already have a delivery mechanism granted by the government without cost and capable of bypassing the cable system altogether."[41] The court seemed to be saying that regulation of cable is permissible if it is specific, narrow, and clearly drawn.

In a case that was rendered moot while on appeal because the franchise was awarded to another company, the court affirmed the concept of public access television:

If cable is to become a constructive force in our national life, it must be open to all Americans. There must be relatively easy access . . . for those who wish to promote their ideas, state their views, or sell their goods and services. [referring to leased access] . . . This *unfettered flow of information is central to freedom of speech and freedom of the press which have been described correctly as the freedom upon which all of our other rights depend.*[42]

Public access television was again in the courts in 1987 when a U.S. District Court heard *Erie Telecommunications v. City of Erie.* The Act's public access television rules were challenged on First and Fourteenth Amendment grounds. The court quoted at length the discussion held in Congress before enacting the 1984 Cable Act, stating:

This Court is convinced that *access requirements further secure the foundation upon which the [F]irst [A]mendment is grounded—promotion of a marketplace of ideas.* . . . Access requirements clearly further the substantial governmental interest of making cable television available for the dissemination of ideas by the general citizenry. . . .

Admittedly, access requirements limit the editorial discretion which cable operators hold over the content of their broadcasts. However, the Court concludes that this infringement is justifiable in light of the regulatory interest held by franchise authorities. . . . The City's imposition of access requirements constitutes a regulation which satisfies each of the elements demanded by the *United States v. O'Brien* opinion.[43]

The court went on the say that it was important that the cable operator still had editorial control over a "substantial majority" of the cable system, and therefore the access requirement imposed only minimally on the cable operator's First Amendment rights. This case was affirmed by the court.[44]

CABLE TELEVISION CONSUMER PROTECTION AND COMPETITION ACT OF 1992

The objectives of the Cable Television Consumer Protection and Competition Act of 1992 (1992 Cable Act), which amended parts of the 1984 Cable Act (and amended the Communication Act of 1934), were the following:

1. To promote the availability to the public of a diversity of views and information through cable television and other video distribution media.
2. To rely on the marketplace, to the maximum extent feasible, to achieve that availability.
3. To ensure that cable operators continue to expand, where economically justified, their capacity and the programs offered over their cable systems.

4. To ensure that consumer interests are protected in receipt of cable service where cable television systems are not subject to effective competition.

5. To ensure that cable television operators do not have undue market power vis-à-vis video programmers and consumers.[45]

The 1992 Cable Act also added language that allows franchisers to require not only PEG access channel capacity but also facilities and financial support as part of their negotiated agreements. Sec. 541(a)(4)(B) states, "In awarding a franchise, the franchising authority—may require adequate assurance that the cable operator will provide adequate public, educational, and governmental access channel capacity, facilities, or financial support."[46] This served further to endorse the idea and reality of public access television.

The 1992 Cable Act also reinstated the must-carry rules and required direct broadcast satellite (DBS) providers to devote 4 to 7 percent of their channel capacity for "noncommercial programming of an educational or informational nature."[47] The must-carry rules were again challenged in the courts and ultimately were ruled constitutional.[48] A difficulty resulting from the must-carry rules for public access is that the cable companies can use must-carry as an excuse for not carrying public access channels. The must-carry rules require cable companies to carry all the local broadcast stations on their system, and therefore, the cable companies reason, there are not enough channels left for public access.[49]

Although the DBS regulations were challenged in the courts, this part of the 1992 Cable Act was upheld and the FCC began implementing rulemaking in mid-1997. Feeling that the new cable rules put them at a competitive disadvantage, the cable companies urged the FCC to impose the same rules on their satellite competitors as had been imposed on cable, including must-carry, program access, and public, educational and governmental access.[50]

Perhaps the most significant difference between the Cable Acts of 1984 and 1992 is that while the earlier legislation granted immunity to cable operators if they transmitted obscene material over PEG or leased access, the 1992 Cable Act took away this legal shield. Sec. 10(c) of the 1992 Cable Act states: "[T]he FCC shall promulgate such regulation as may be necessary to enable a cable operator of a cable system to prohibit the use, on such system, of any channel capacity of any public, educational, or governmental access facility for any programming which contains obscene material, sexually explicit conduct, or material soliciting or promoting unlawful conduct."[51] Cable operators could now be held responsible for any obscene programming on PEG access channels. The 1992 Cable Act allows cable operators to prohibit public access television facilities from being used for indecent or obscene programming and removed the immunity for cable operators who transmit indecent or obscene programs over their systems.[52]

Almost immediately after the passage of the 1992 Cable Act a series of complaints were filed by cable operators about various sections of the act, including PEG access and obscenity on access.[53] Several of these cases were consolidated into one—*Daniels Cablevision v. United States*. In its decision in this case, the U.S. District Court said:

The PEG . . . access provisions were enacted to serve a significant regulatory interest, *viz.*, affording speakers with lesser market appeal access to the nation's most pervasive video distribution technology. Enabling a broad range of speakers to reach a television audience that otherwise would never hear them is an appropriate goal and a legitimate exercise of federal legislative power. . . . Nor do the PEG . . . access provisions overreach. PEG use is negotiable.[54]

Using the *O'Brien* test, the court declared that PEG access does not violate the cable operators' First Amendment rights because: (1) [the] statute is content neutral, (2) [the] statute was enacted in order to enable [a] broad range of speakers to reach [a] television audience that otherwise would never hear them, which is [an] appropriate goal and legitimate exercise of federal legislative power, and (3) [the] statute does not overreach.[55]

Daniels also challenged the obscenity regulation, observing that the cable operators had no control over the programming shown on PEG access channels. The court noted that

The plaintiffs and the American Civil Liberties Union, as amicus, contend that potential liability for obscenity carried on PEG and leased access channels impermissibly burdens speech by creating an unacceptable incentive to operator self-censorship. Without immunity, they argue, operators will be forced to screen their PEG and leased access programming for material that might be deemed obscene, and the more timorous among them will become so apprehensive that they will voluntarily refuse to carry controversial programming that might nevertheless enjoy full constitutional protection.[56]

The court concluded that no one has a constitutional right to immunity in this area and that Congress can grant that immunity or take it away as it wishes.[57] The court upheld the 1992 Cable Act as written.

In another major case concerning this issue, *Alliance for Community Media v. FCC*, the U.S. Court of Appeals for the District of Columbia ruled that "provisions of the [1992 Cable Act], and implementing regulations, authorizing cable operators to ban indecent programming from leased access and public access channels violate the First Amendment."[58] The court said, "[N]ot only does the First Amendment prohibit the government from banning all indecent speech from access channels, it also prevents the government from deputizing cable operators with the power to effect such a ban."[59] After the three-judge panel of the court handed down its judgment, the FCC requested that the court rehear the case *in banc*.[60] The decision was overturned by the entire eleven-member court in June 1995 on the grounds that the regulations did not violate the First Amendment and so were constitutional.

The Alliance for Community Media appealed to the U.S. Supreme Court where the case was combined with *Denver Area Educational Telecommunications Consortium v. FCC* and argued in February 1996. The Supreme Court ruled that the section of the 1992 Cable Act that allows the cable operator to censor indecent programming on *leased* access channels was constitutional. The Court ruled, however, that the remaining two sections under consideration—requiring cable operators to segregate and block indecent programming on leased channels and to censor indecent programming on PEG channels—violated the First Amendment and were not constitutional.[61]

As to the rationale for allowing censoring on leased channels and not allowing censoring on PEG channels, the Court cited four differences between PEG access and leased access. The first was the historical publicness of the PEG channels and the previous absence of editorial control by the cable company. The second difference stemmed from the institutional nature of public access television. These channels "are subject to complex supervisory systems of various sorts. . . . This system of public, private, and mixed nonprofit elements, through its supervising boards and nonprofit or governmental access managers, can set programming policy and approve or disapprove particular programming sources. And this system can police that policy, by, for example, requiring indemnification by programmers, certification of compliance with local standards, time segregation, adult content advisories, or even prescreening individual programs."[62] Because most access organizations already have policies and procedures in place to manage this type of programming, the Court ruled that federal regulations were not necessary. The third difference cited by the Court was "the existence of a system aimed at encouraging and securing programming that the community considers valuable strongly suggests that a 'cable operator's veto' is less likely to be necessary to achieve the statute's basic objective, protecting children, than a similar veto in the context of leased channels."[63] And the fourth difference was that there was no compelling need, nationally, to protect children from significantly harmful materials on PEG access. "The upshot in respect to the public access channels," said the Court, "is a law that could radically change present programming-related relationships among local community and nonprofit supervising boards and access managers, which relationships are established through municipal law, regulation, and contract. . . . [G]iven present supervisory mechanisms, the need for this particular provision, aimed directly at public access channels, is not obvious."[64] In making its decision, the Court considered information from many public access television advocates and supporters.[65] Public access television remains a free speech forum.

TELECOMMUNICATIONS ACT OF 1996 AND PUBLIC ACCESS TELEVISION

The Telecommunications Act of 1996 (1996 Act) required the FCC to adopt rules that would extend PEG access provisions to "open video systems" (OVS) or others without obtaining a cable franchise. An OVS is a cable television or video delivery system provided by the telephone company. There had been some trepidation among public access television and cable administrators that OVS operators would not have to comply with PEG rules and regulations. The 1996 Act helped to assuage these fears. Although it does not, however, require telecommunications companies providing OVS to have a franchise agreement with the local municipality, there is still some confusion as to how this new rule will be implemented. The FCC clarified somewhat the PEG on OVS section of the 1996 Act in August 1996. According to this rulemaking, the OVS operator will have to match the level of support the local cable company provides for public access television. Rather than splitting the cable operator's current commitment, OVS regulations will result in a doubling of resources for public access television. Certain aspects of this rule have been appealed, however, and were pending before the U.S. Court of Appeals for the Fifth Circuit as this book went to press.[66]

In addition, the Act allows franchising authorities to impose a fee up to, or equal to, the franchise fees the local cable operator is required to pay. Section 506 of the 1996 Act permits cable operators to censor obscenity, indecency, or nudity on public access television programs, much as the 1992 Cable Act did. However, since the 1992 rules were invalidated by the Supreme Court in *Denver Area*, this section is not enforceable insofar as it extends to programming that is not obscene. The FCC acknowledged this when it issued a *Memorandum and Order* in May 1997 stating: "Finally, as a result of the Court's decision that Section 10(c) [of the 1992 Cable Act] is unconstitutional, we will amend Section 76.702. Insofar as the 1996 Act grants to the operator the right to refuse to transmit indecent public access programming, it apparently conflicts with the Court's decision in *Denver Consortium* that *cable operators may not prohibit 'the tramsmission of "patently offensive" sex-related material' over public access channels.*"[67]

In an interesting twist, New York Mayor Rudy Giuliani attempted to take away two of the five public access channels in Manhattan in late 1996 to make room for two news channels on the Time Warner cable system serving Manhattan. Time Warner had refused to allow the news channels on their system. The appeals court ruled that public access channels are reserved for use by the public, not for commercial news services.[68]

CONCLUSION

The 1992 Cable Act reaffirmed Congress' support of public access television. In *Daniels*, the court reaffirmed the court's belief that public access television does not pose a constitutional question. Because the government used *O'Brien* to allow franchisers to require PEG access as part of franchise agreements, the 1984 and 1992 Cable Acts appear to be constitutionally sound.

At the current time, the concept of public access television is not being challenged in the courts. Even if there are sporadic lawsuits, it appears that the future existence of public access television will not be decided in the courts, but in the chambers of local municipalities and other community forums. The 1984 and 1992 Cable Acts allow franchisers, usually municipalities, to require public access of the cable operator as part of the franchise agreement, and the 1996 Act extends PEG requirements to OVS. Municipalities, though, are unlikely to require cable operators to provide public access cable television unless individuals and the community request it. And even then it may be an uphill battle, because the cable company can pass expenses on to subscribers.[69] This means that the greatest threat to the future of public access television is less likely to come from legal challenges than from the indifference of local citizens and competing demands for funds from local governmental entities. The laws create an environment with certain safeguards, but provide no guarantee of funding. If the public does not actively lobby for public access television and usher it into existence, all the years of legislative and regulatory progress will have been for naught.

NOTES

1. 38 FCC 683, 685 (1965).
2. 391 US 367, 377 (1968).
3. 392 US 157, 172, 178 (1968).
4. 395 US 367, 390 (1969).
5. 15 FCC 2d 417, 422 (1968).
6. 25 FCC 2d 38, 41 (1970).
7. Ibid., 48–49.
8. 31 FCC 2d 115, 128 (1971).
9. Ibid.
10. Ibid., 130.
11. Ibid., 131.
12. 406 US 649, 667 (1972).
13. Ibid., 670.

14. 36 FCC 2d 143, 190–91 (1972). Note that the use of the channel was free, but production costs were not. However, it is these production costs that prevented people from participating in television production. Television production requires expensive equipment and at this time the cost was prohibitive for most people.

15. Ibid., 194
16. 418 US 241, 258 (1974).
17. 523 F2d 1344, 1351 (1975).
18. *Buckley v. Valeo*, 424 US 1, 48–49 (1976) (citations omitted).
19. 59 FCC 2d 294, 296 (1976).
20. Ibid., 298.
21. Ibid., 299.
22. 533 F2d 601, 615 (1976).
23. 567 F2d 9, 13 (1977).
24. 573 F2d 765, 767 (1978).
25. 406 US 649 (1972).
26. 440 US 689, 708 (1979).
27. Ibid., 713–14 (citations omitted).
28. 485 FSupp. 1035, 1040 (1980).
29. 555 FSupp. 1164, 1172 (1982).
30. Ibid., 1352.

31. *Missouri Knights of the Ku Klux Klan v. City of Kansas City, Missouri*, 723 FSupp. 1347, 1352 (W.D. Mo. 1989).

32. Ibid., 1354.

33. *Perry Education Association v. Perry Local Educators' Association*, 460 US 37, 45 (1984).

34. 909 SW2d 264 (Texas Ct. of Appeals) (1995); "Public Access Cable Show Obscenity Convictions Upheld: Court: 'Safe-Sex' Video not Educational," *News Media & the Law* 20, no. 1 (Winter 1996): 38; and W. Bernard Lukenbill, "Eroticized, AIDs-HIV Information on Public-Access Television: A Study of Obscenity, State Censorship and Cultural Resistance," *AIDS Education and Prevention* 10, no. 3 (1998): 230.

35. *Perry Education Association v. Perry Local Educators' Association*, 460 US 37, 45 (1983).

36. Ibid., 55.

37. 467 US 691, 701 (1984).

38. *U.S. Code*, vol. 47, sec. 521 (1984).

39. Ibid.

40. 768 F2d 1434, 1438 (1985).

41. Ibid., 1452–53.

42. *Berkshire Cablevision v. Burke*, 571 FSupp. 986, 987 (1983).

43. 659 FSupp. 580, 599 (1987) (citations omitted).

44. Ibid., 601.

45. J.P. Coustel, "New Rules for Cable Television in the United States: Reducing the Market Power of Cable Operators," *Telecommunications Policy* (April 1993), 214.

46. *U.S. Code*, vol. 47, sec. 541 (a)(4)(B) (1992).

47. *U.S. Code*, vol 47, sec. 335(b)(1).

48. *Turner Broadcasting System, Inc. v. FCC*, 512 US 1145; and *Turner Broadcasting System, Inc. v. FCC*, 117 SCt 1174.

49. TCI Cable of Westchester planned to reassign its public access channel because of the must-carry rules. See "TCI Cable Makes Official Cutback in Public Access," *New York Times*, 7 April 1996, sec. WC, p. 13.

50. *Daniels Cablevision, Inc. v. U.S.*, 835 FSupp. 1 (D.D.C. 1993); and Chris McConnell, "Cable Backs Public Interest Rules—for DBS," *Broadcasting and Cable* 127, no. 19 (5 May 1997): 21–24.

51. Ibid., 1486.

52. *U.S. Code*, vol 47, sec. 558 (1988).

53. Nicholas P. Miller and Joseph Van Eaton, "A Review of Developments in Cases Defining the Scope of the First Ammendment Rights of Cable Television Operators," *Cable Television Law* 2 (1993): 298.

54. 835 FSupp. 1, 6–7 (DDC 1993) (citations omitted).

55. Ibid.

56. Ibid., 11.

57. Ibid.

58. 10 F3d 812, 817 (DC Cir 1993).

59. Ibid., 815.

60. *In banc* refers to the entire eleven-member Court of Appeals.

61. 116 SCt 2374, 2394 (1996).

62. Ibid., 2395.

63. Ibid., 2396.

64. Ibid., 2397.

65. Ibid., 2396–97. Comments noted by the Court in its decision were from Patricia Aufderheide; Boston Community Access and Programming Foundation; Metropolitan Area Communications Commission; Waycross Community Television; Columbus Community Cable Access; City of St. Paul; Erik Molberg, Public Access Coordinator, Ft. Wayne, IN; Defiance Community Television; Nutmeg Public Access Television; Boston Community Access and Programming Foundation; Staten Island Community Television; Cambridge Community Television; Columbus Community Cable Access; and Cincinnati Community Video.

66. *Telecommunications Act of 1996*, U.S. Code Supplement II, vol. 47, sec. 531–59 (1996).

67. MM Docket No. 92-258 (slip op. At 4–5), May 7, 1997.

68. Donna Petrozzello, "Time Warner Wins NYC Cable News Fight," *Broadcasting and Cable* 127, no. 28 (7 July 1997): 5.

69. Andy Newman, "More than Television," *New York Times*, 1 January 1996, New Jersey edition, p. 1.

3

Current Status of Public Access Television

Public access cable television today consists of approximately two thousand centers[1] in the United States producing more than fifteen-thousand hours of new local programming every week. That is more programming than is produced by NBC, CBS, ABC, FOX, and PBS combined. According to a 1992 survey, however, fewer than 20 percent of United States communities are served by public access television. Although public access television in the United States is funded primarily by the cable companies, local management is handled by various entities, including nonprofit agencies, local governments, high schools, and colleges.[2]

ORGANIZATION AND MANAGEMENT

Most often public access television is managed in one of three ways: by the local government, by the cable operator, or by a nonprofit agency created for that purpose. When managed by the cable company, public access television tends to be neglected. This is predictable since, from the cable company's point of view, the more public access television is used, the more it costs. It makes good business sense for the cable company to maintain a minimum level of service to hold down costs. When public access television is managed by the local governmental entity, the public access television budget is subject to municipal budget fluctuations and changes in the political winds. When public access is operated by local government, programming is inevitably linked to other official policies or programs. Citizens tend to hold their elected officials generally accountable for programming decisions made by the public access television organization when in reality the officials have little control. Because of these

Table 3.1
Types of Management Structures of Public Access Centers in the United States

Type of Management Structure	Percentage of Centers
Local cable company	37
Nonprofit	26
Local governmental entity	22
Educational institution	13
Library	1
Other	1

difficulties—lack of promotion and outreach by the cable company, annual budgetary constraints, and the inability of elected officials to exercise control of programming content—the nonprofit model has proven to be most advantageous for public access television management.

A nonprofit organization is managed by a board of directors composed of local citizens who are volunteers and have a stake in the success of the organization. Because of this personal commitment, they tend to do a better job of educating the community about public access television, setting priorities, addressing the diversity of the community, and raising money. In addition, they are in a better position to deal with controversial programming, if necessary. According to the *Community Media Resource Directory*, nonprofits and government entities manage about half the centers, over a third are managed by the local cable company, and a little more that 10 percent are managed by educational institutions.[3] (See Table 3.1.)

FACILITIES

Public access television facilities run the gamut from the regal to the humble. Predictably, larger cities such as New York have some of the more sophisticated operations; the Manhattan Neighborhood Network is a located in an historic former movie studio. In smaller cities and rural towns, the extent of the public access operation is more likely to be a camcorder and a playback deck in the office at the local cable company.[4]

Even within a particular region served by a single cable operator, the range can be enormous. For example, Cablevision of New Jersey, one of forty-seven cable carriers in the state, provides minimum public access service to many of the municipalities it serves. After a protracted legal battle, however, Cablevision provided the city of Bayonne with the funds for a new studio and the equipment to produce an impressive array of local programs. At the other end of the state, a cable carrier called C-Tec provides subscribers in the Princeton area with six twenty-four-hour access channels as well as two-way cables for future interactive programming.[5]

Additional examples include Citizens TV in New Haven, Connecticut, with a 5,348 square foot facility; Nutmeg Television in Farmington, Connecticut, with a

1,300 square foot facility; Mission Viejo, California, jointly operated with the Saddleback Valley Unified School District and housed in the high school; and Fort Wayne, Indiana, located in the public library.[6]

Each public access television center typically has a studio with two or three cameras mounted on tripods, a switcher, an audio board with inputs for several microphones, a cassette player and/or CD player, a character generator (CG) for graphics, and an incoming telephone line. Some studios have much more and many have less. For example, the facility in Boston has everything listed above as well as a second, smaller studio with duplicates of everything—cameras, switcher, audio, CG, and phone line—organized so that one person can produce a television program without needing a crew (people to operate the cameras, switcher, audio, and character generator). Boston Community Television also has a salaried staff to train and assist anyone who wants to become a producer. At the other end of the spectrum, public access television in Bellhaven, North Carolina, consists of a room at the cable company for a studio, a camcorder and a playback deck. The channel airs a bulletin board most of the time, but has gone live for Halloween, Christmas, and the Fourth of July.

In addition to a studio setup, most public access television centers also have field equipment consisting of portable cameras, tripods, light kits, and microphones that can be checked out, as well as one or more video editing stations where producers can edit their shows. Many centers also provide dubbing services for their producers, either for a fee or at no cost. Public access television centers that are responsible for playback of tapes will also have some kind of playback system and equipment to transfer the video and audio signal to the cable company.

The extent and quality of the facility and equipment of each public access television center varies and is dependent upon the amount of funding each center receives from its funding source. As one might suppose, the more money a center has, the better the facility and equipment tend to be.[7]

Because public access television centers need to be available to the public, most are open at least eight to twelve hours a day, six days a week. There are centers that stay open longer, but usually hours of operation are a function of how much funding they receive; the more hours the center is open, the more staff is required. The busiest time for most public access television centers is during the late afternoon and evening hours and on Saturdays, when most people have time to devote to production. Almost all public access producers are volunteers. In fact, most producers find that their shows take somewhat longer to produce than they had anticipated and also require money for videotape and other supplies.

PROGRAMMING AND PRODUCERS

There is no "profile" for a public access television producer. The people who use the forum include local activists, senior citizens, elected officials, teenagers and business people, among others. It is impossible to make any general about so varied a group. Perhaps all that can be said about these individuals is that they recognize the value of noncommercial, uncensored television. It is equally difficult to categorize the content of public access television shows, which ranges from silly to sublime, serious to sensational. It is the public nature of public access television that allows for an extremely diverse group of producers and programs.

Citizens TV, or CTV, consists of three channels in New Haven, Connecticut, that provide "programming twenty-four hours a day, seven days a week. All their programs are produced by amateurs with training provided by CTV. The production staff is all volunteer." At CTV there are about "eighty producers [who] deliver programming on a weekly basis and one hundred and fifty more [who] occasionally make programs. They are allowed one hour a week of programming time." This structure is replicated in public access television centers across the country. Public access channels cablecast programming produced by local producers, and many centers will cablecast "imported" programming—programming produced elsewhere, but "sponsored" (brought in for cablecast) by a local resident. When there is no programming being cablecast, most centers put on a community bulletin board (comprised of computer-generated text and graphics) containing announcements about upcoming community events.[8]

There are a multitude of other public access television shows covering a wide range of topics in over two thousand communities in the United States. This programming varies from locale to locale yet is also remarkably similar in many ways. As noted in Chapter 1, one of the best examples of public access television programming is also one of the oldest. "Alternative Views," which began in 1978, is still being produced intermittently in Austin, Texas.[9] In Fort Wayne, Indiana, the top-rated public access television shows, according to a telephone survey completed by the Allen County Public Library, are: "Speak Out," "Komet Hockey," "The Uncle Ducky Show," "Situation Number Nine," "Highway Videos," "YWCA Body Shop," and "Raiders of Access." In Grand Rapids, Michigan, the Grand Rapids Cable Access Center (GRTV) includes in its regular schedule "The Job Show," "Healing the Ancient Arts," and "Yo! Grand Rapids." In Middlebury, Vermont, two community news shows, "Front Page" and "In View," are cablecast regularly, as is "Community Dialogue." Many public access television shows are not part of a series. Two of these single-shot shows are "The Artist Joseph Hahn in Middlebury" and "Art and the Rosenbergs." Middlebury also imports programming such as "Alternative Views" from Austin, Texas, "Bonjour," a French-Canadian show from Manchester, New Hampshire, and "Journey," a show produced by the Roman Catholic Diocese in Burlington, Vermont.[10]

Newark, New Jersey boasts an impressive array of public access programs. There is "Extra Help," a popular biweekly call-in show on which local school-teachers field student questions related to their homework assignments; "Exposure," an acclaimed local arts program; "State of the Union," a labor-oriented show on current events; and "White-Collar Crime Report," which attempts to keep viewers abreast of boardroom misdeeds.[11]

Public access television has also become a resource for local civic organizations. Nonprofits as well as social service organizations have begun to see the value of public access television. (See Table 3.2 for a sample of groups across the country who are using public access television.) To help facilitate the use of public access television by nonprofit organizations, the Benton Foundation, a national philanthropic organization providing support to nonprofits, has issued several publications on how to use video to promote a nonprofit organization. Two of these publications, *Cable Access* and *Making Video*, are guides for nonprofit organizations on producing video programs for public access television.

Around the country, public access television is used by minority groups to foster understanding and promote community. In Lynn, Massachusetts, "Cosmos," a weekly half-hour Spanish-language show, "explain[s] local and world affairs to Spanish-speaking people in the region." Pedro Diaz Hernandez, a Massachusetts representative and reporter for *Presencia*, a Hispanic newspaper, is the host and producer of the show, along with his wife, Altagracia Diaz, and their children. "Haiti Tele-Magazine Network," which airs weekly, attempts "to bring homesick immigrants the news from their homeland while providing instruction and advice on how to get along in America." In Pocatello, Idaho, "LaVoz Latina," a live Spanish-language talk show, has been in production almost every Sunday since 1982. This show has made a big difference for the Hispanic community in southeast Idaho. Local Iranians produce a show in Dallas, Texas to preserve their culture and help foster community among the local Iranian population.[12]

Jim Russell, Assistant Operations Director at Whitewater Community Television in Wayne County, Indiana, reports a variety of original programming at WCTV, including "Cuffs," "Exciting Explorations," "Focus on the Arts," "Health Forum," "Health Call," and "Help the Animals." "Cuffs" was started by two local police officers to profile local individuals who are wanted by the police for nonpayment of fines, check deception, drug trafficking, and failure to pay child support. The program shows pictures of the wanted individuals while the police officers read information about the case. The show has expanded to include segments on unsolved crimes and to show the duties of various classes of police officers. The success of the show is indicated by the fact that 74 percent of the cases that have been highlighted on the show have been cleared. On "Exciting Explorations," a local woman takes children on field trips to explore different places in the community; they have visited several museums and a radio station. Once a month on "Health Call," a doctor answers health questions from the public in a live, call-in format. "Help the Animals" is produced by volunteers from one of the local animal shelters and features animals the shelter currently has available for adoption. In addition, the show covers topics such as spaying and neutering pets, grooming, and obedience training.[13] Another show called "Contra Costa County's Deadbeat Parents" "exposes parents who are delinquent in paying child support."[14] After having difficulty recruiting volunteers, the Great Neck Vigilant Fire Company created a public service announcement just for that

Table 3.2
Sample of Nonprofit Organizations and the Public Access Television Shows They Produce

Organization & Location	Title of Show	Description of Show
Wrightwood Improvement Association Chicago, Illinois	"Home Equity"	neighborhood association used public access TV to publicize an impending referendum
Milwaukee Audubon Society Milwaukee, Wisconsin	"Milwaukee Audubon Presents" and "Earthcare"	Audubon Society uses public access television to publicize environmental issues
Roger B. Chaffee Planetarium Grand Rapids, Michigan	"Neptune Encounter"	cablecast a program about Voyager 2 spacecraft
Foxborough, Massachusetts Council for Human Services Foxborough, Massachusetts	"Auction I" and "Auction II"	cablecasts its annual auction
Good Samaritan Hospital and Medical Center Portland, Oregon	"Health Visions"	teaches viewers how to cook for the diabetic, clean up cholesterol, break the cycle of PMS, et.al.
Los Angeles Jazz Society Los Angeles, California	"Jazz in Review"	spotlights jazz, musicians, and the Jazz Society
United Way/Neighbors Helping Neighbors, Inc. San Luis Obispo County, California	"Good Neighbor Community Outreach"	profiles different community agencies
American Association of Retired Persons, Inc. Area VII Dallas, Texas	"Senior Speak Out"	highlights AARP events and involves seniors in production
Northern Virginia Youth Services Fairfax, Virginia	"Focus on Youth"	addresses critical issues facing today's youth
Little City Foundation Palatine, Illinois	"Given Opportunities"	mentally handicapped people produce a show to challenge and change people's attitudes
League of Women Voters Bucks County, Pennsylvania	"At Issue"	ongoing documentary series on local issues

Source: Margie Nicholson, "Cable Access," *Strategic Communications for Nonprofits*, Washington, DC: Benton Foundation, 1992.

purpose. Three of the company's volunteer firefighters got together and "wrote, produced, directed, filmed, and edited the spots." "The firefighters experience before making the spots was zero. . . . The three learned television skills at Great Neck–North Shore (Long Island, New York) Public Access Television." The National Federation of Local Cable Programmers (now the Alliance for Community Media) judged these spots the most outstanding in the whole country for that year.[15]

Public access is used by many communities to promote civic awareness. In Macomb County, Michigan, election results were simultaneously transmitted via the local public access channel and the Internet for the November 1997 elections. Information transmitted from the clerk's office via the Internet and displayed on public access was updated every two minutes. In at least five states (New York, Oregon, Michigan, Rhode Island, and Washington) legislators are allowed to produce programs informing voters about what is happening in state government. A New York assemblyman produces "Assembly Calendar"; "Meet the Speaker" is produced in Rhode Island; and "Legislative Update" in Washington State allows legislators three- to five-minute shows. In Philadelphia, the police department has been producing programs on public access for six years. They have produced three different types of shows: a live call-in show, a talk show, and a fugitive-style show. (An article about how to produce these types of shows was published in the June 1997 issue of *The FBI Law Enforcement Bulletin*.)[16]

Many public access television shows are standard interview/talk shows, but in each community they are focused on the people and issues relevant to their community. "Good About Brockton" highlights individuals and organizations who make a difference in Brockton, Massachusetts. According to its producer, "Speaking of Summit" is "television for the people, by the people, and about the people who are my friends and neighbors. We cover ourselves!" The show invites the mayor and other local government officials, representatives of city agencies, and members of nonprofit groups to talk about what is happening in Summit, New Jersey. "Sacramento Soapbox" is a "weekly talk show on local, national, and international political issues, from a progressive point of view." Producer John Webb is a video production instructor who has been producing public access television shows for twelve years. Greensboro Community Television collaborated with the local public library and the historical museum to produce "Community Voices," an oral history project that will become an interactive, multimedia archive of interviews, photos, graphics, and writing. A public screening of the entire series will be aired on the public access channel when the project is completed and the CD-ROM disks will be available for use at the public library.[17]

Serving a large and diverse population, Chicago Access Network (CAN TV), offers over 540 hours of programming weekly, including as many as twelve hundred different shows. There is an alternative talk show called "Caviar & Grits," which features five men talking about subjects of interest to Chicagoans from national politics to local television. The show was described by a reporter for the *Chicago Tribune* as "five guys chewing the fat at a barber shop on a Saturday afternoon."[18] Another program offers an interactive call-in data bank, whereby viewers can access hundreds of "pages" or bulletins with information on jobs, education, health, entertainment and other topics. Other offerings available to Chicagoans on public access have been less mundane. "Songsation" featured a drawing of a "wild-eyed creature 'interviewing' a man describing works at an art gallery, a song entitled 'Eck,' about falling into a sewer, and another drawing named 'Dr. Toilet,' 'chatting up' an alternative band." The "Surprise Show" featured a woman sitting in a cornfield talking about her newborn son for a half-hour.[19]

Some public access channels have also used innovative scheduling techniques that would never be possible on commercial outlets. One such unusual programming approach was utilized by a rural system out of Portland, Oregon where, each weekend, one program is run continuously for two days. Channel spokesman Reuben Contreras told *Television Quarterly* that this was a way of bringing the program to the viewers, whenever they had time to watch it, rather than putting the burden on them to find it.[20]

Many public access television shows are showcases for local talent. These include: "Cafe with Andre," featuring art, poetry, music, dance, and coffeemaking out of Summit, New Jersey; "Hometown Showcase" in Dayton, Ohio; "Young Chicago," featuring local teen talent as well as issues affecting the city's youth; and "USA Kids Today," produced by kids ages six through fourteen from Dayton, Ohio, with help from Karen Harker.[21] A consummate example of showcasing local talent is "Two on the Aisle," in which two former newspaper critics review Broadway and off-Broadway theatre productions. Both are just two of an estimated five hundred self-styled personalities who appear on the four public access channels operated by Manhattan Cable.[22]

Much of the eccentricity on public access television flows from the shows' producer and/or hosts. Two producers who represent part of this range of diversity are Ira Gallen, producer and star of the show "Biograph Days, Biograph Nights," and Glendora Buell, producer and star of "A Chat With Glendora." Gallen's show is "an affectionate glance at the television programs and commercials of the 1950s and 1960s." The thirty-minute program airs seven days a week and has become a cult favorite.[23] "A Chat With Glendora" has been called more of a monologue than a talk show. Buell's show airs weekly and consists of her reading transcripts of her court cases, and attacking judges, politicians, and the legal system.[24]

Lorna Hawkins began producing her public access show in Los Angeles as a way for herself and others to deal with grief. "Drive-by Agony" first aired after her son was shot and killed in a drive-by shooting. After three years of producing and hosting the show, her other son was shot and killed by a gang, in an incident unrelated to her show or her other son's murder. Her show has helped her keep going, as well as providing a forum for others who have lost loved ones to acts of violence.[25]

Producer Art Fein has hosted four hundred episodes of "Poker's Party," about "[a] rock 'n' roll subculture called 'roots' music: relentless, rollicking stuff that ranges from 1940s 'jump blues' to the rockabilly music played by Elvis Presley and a score of Elvis-imitating hillbillies in the mid- to late-1950s." His show airs on public access channels in Los Angeles, New York, and Austin, Texas.[26] "The Waldrop Family Sings" is "a homespun half-hour of original hymns, prayer and inspiration." The show is shot at the family home and airs in east San Fernando Valley, Santa Clarita, and parts of Ventura County, California; Tucson, Arizona; and Nashville, Tennessee. Mary Ellen and Will Tracy produce "Sabrina On," one of the "best-known public access television programs in the Los Angeles area." The show features "Sabrina" (Mary Ellen) as a priestess "[who] preaches about such metaphysical matters as how women can help themselves achieve orgasm."[27] John Crean's "At Home on the Range" is "a cooking show that in the past year has become an Orange County cable TV sensation, watched by college kids and society folks alike." The show, part cooking, part comedy, is produced and cohosted by Barbara Venezia. Taped four times a month before a live audience, it is cablecast over all ten Orange County systems. And in Los Angeles, Joey Buttafucco attempts to remake/cash in on his image by hosting a thirty-minute show that he describes as a "forum for those who have 'been screwed by their lawyers, screwed by society, screwed by the judicial system."[28]

At least two Manhattan Neighborhood Network shows have been picked up by MTV. "Squirt TV" features the host sitting in bed talking about music, news, and anything else. A combination talk show and amateur hour, "Oddville TV" has featured, among other things, a human bowling ball and a rap-dancing grandmother.[29]

Public access television programming takes many different forms, and every year the Alliance for Community Media sponsors the Hometown Video Festival to celebrate the best of community programming. Because of the diversity of public access television programming, the festival selects programs in forty-four different categories. Winners are honored and receive a plaque or certificate at the annual awards ceremony at the ACM National Conference, held every July. A compilation tape of the winners is distributed each year, as is a directory of the winners' show titles, description of the show, and names and addresses.

CONTROVERSIAL PROGRAMMING

For all of its amateurism and eclecticism, most of the fare on public access falls well within acceptable norms. But there are a few shows that bring an outcry from local viewers because of their controversial nature. Shows that fall into this category tend to be either tasteless, indecent, or involve controversial social or political content. When public access television directors were asked in a survey about controversial programming, most respondents offered the following types as examples: sex and health education, particularly AIDS education; topical call-in; programs featuring political fringe opinions; programs featuring cultural minorities, especially young people; and experimental videos.[30]

One of the mildest of these was an hour-long program featuring text only. The show consisted of the words 'Hemp, Hemp, Hurray!' against a background of changing colors, circles and squares, accompanied by cartoon music. Some viewers were upset about this overt endorsement of an illegal substance, and especially about the timing of the cablecast of the show—it was shown in the afternoon. However, the cable company, which administers public access television, considered it artistic expression and defended itself by saying that "public access programming allows wide freedom of expression except in cases of extreme obscenity or explicit sexuality."[31]

Another controversy arose in Seattle about a show in a local series called "Political Playhouse." Very similar to "Alternative Views" in its mission and content, the show is considered an unrestricted, free-thought forum. But one special edition, which aired in June, 1994, differed from other offerings in the series in two respects. First, the show was considerably longer than usual, at four-and-a-half hours. Second, all but four of the participants, including the technical crew and approximately fifteen cast members, did the show in the nude "to protest the notion that the human body is inherently obscene." Within a few minutes after the show went on the air, TCI Cable, the local carrier, was deluged with phone calls. The program, which was picked up by several public access television stations in other cities, touched off a firestorm of protest, editorializing, and commentary. Similarly, a program from Virginia entitled "Gay Fairfax" received a great deal of publicity, much of it negative, for "sexually explicit" depictions and references. Another show, "Dan Savage and the Sex Kittens," cablecast in Raleigh, North Carolina in 1995, featured scenes from local striptease joints, among other field trips. All of these shows elicited a storm of protest from viewers and nonviewers alike.[32]

One of the most notorious public access television programs was "The Great Satan at Large," a live call-in show produced in Tucson, Arizona. The show, which appeared in 1991, featured "exposed genitalia, the fondling of a young woman's breasts by a cast member, masturbation by a cast member, nudity, film clips showing mutilation and real or simulated murder, and a discussion of bestiality and anal and oral sex by the host, cast and call-in viewers." In this particular instance, the producer was arrested and subsequently suspended from Tucson Community Cable because his show contained illegal acts.[33]

Another program that caused a commotion was "Sick & Wrong," cablecast in New York. During a show in August 1996, the host "cut the heads off three live, bright-green iguanas with a large, serrated kitchen knife." He then pulled their skins off and cooked them on a grill. He was subsequently arrested and charged with three counts of cruelty to animals.[34]

But many public access programs have presented communities with less clear-cut issues relating to decency standards. In *Rees v. State of Texas* (see also Chapter 2), for example, the controversy centered around a three-minute segment of a two-hour program called "Infosex," which offended some viewers but was considered by the producers to be educational advocacy for safe sex practices. The local court found the entire program to be obscene and the Appeals Court upheld the decision.[35]

Not all the controversy revolves around questions of sexuality or indecency. In Grand Rapids, Michigan, a regular series called "Lies of Our Times" has drawn considerable attention for its exposés of inaccuracies and omissions in mainstream media coverage of local, national, and international issues. On several occasions, the show's producers have endorsed sanctuary for Latin American refugees and encouraged blockades of government offices in protest of United States policies in that region. And in Middlebury, Vermont, a show called "RU486 Legal Forum," discussed the possible introduction of the "abortion pill" to the United States and served as a lightning rod for a heated war of words between many area groups with an interest in reproductive rights.[36]

In addition to tastelessness, indecency, and other controversial issues, hate speech also brings an outcry from local viewers. "Race and Reason," the Ku Klux Klan show mentioned in Chapter 1, is the best known example of a show in the hate speech category. This show is well-known because KKK members across the country obtain copies of the show, take the tapes to their local public access television center, and request that they be played. Neo-Nazis and White American Skin Heads have aired their programming in Cincinnati, along with other anti-Semitic programming. Response from the community in these cases is usually loud and vociferous, and frequently there are demands made for elimination of the programming and/or the channel. But as noted in Chapter 2, public access television has been recognized as a free speech forum, and as long as the program does not say or portray anything illegal, the show will be aired.[37]

Although controversial programming comprises 1 percent or less of all public access television programming, it is this type of programming that attracts most attention from viewers and elected officials. Most public access television centers do not prescreen tapes lest they be accused of censorship, not to mention the amount of time required for this task. Most centers, however, do require the producer to sign a statement as to the content of the tape and acceptance of their responsibility for the contents. If the producer identifies her tape as being adult-oriented, the tape is scheduled for a late-night time slot.[38]

Media experts generally agree that the best rejoinder to potentially offensive programming is counterprogramming. In those cities where "Race and Reason" has been aired, the most effective response has come from groups such as the National Association for the Advancement of Colored People, the American Jewish Committee, and the Anti-Defamation League of B'nai B'rith, which produced shows of their own to air before and/or after the KKK show.

VIEWERSHIP

There is no equivalent of Nielsen ratings for public access, so there is relatively little hard data regarding viewership, but the outcry whenever a controversial show is cablecast on public access television is one indication that public access television is being watched more than most people realize. Most of the data that does exist has come in the form of community surveys. In a February 11, 1996, *Boston Globe*, story about the growing awareness of community television, Beth Daley reported that "a market analysis was done for the Winthrop business community" that showed 76 percent of the residents watch the public access channel.[39]

Several surveys completed since 1973 have demonstrated an increasing awareness of public access television and an increase in viewership. A summary of these surveys is featured in Table 3.3.[40] In 1985, as part of her doctoral dissertation, Margaret Hardenbergh examined the producers, content, and audiences of four public access channels in Connecticut to determine how well they fulfilled their objective of providing an alternative to commercial television. The study concluded that, to varying degrees, the public access channels functioned as a "mini-medium," presenting content "not normally covered by the mass media." The survey also determined that half the population had watched public access, with 30 percent able to recall a particular program, and that most turned to public access because of the content. Ironically, the Hardenbergh study found that one of the factors limiting unique programming was the pressure that many producers put on themselves "to produce traditional television content in terms of production style."[41]

A national survey conducted by ELRA Group in 1986 showed that almost 19 percent of cable viewers had watched public access television during the previous week. As Atkin and LaRose report, "Community channels do, however, perform consistently better than such satellite-delivered channels as BET, C-SPAN, Financial News Network, PTL, and SPN. (See Table 3.4.) They can even match the performance of Arts and Entertainment, CBN [now The Family Channel] and Lifetime at certain times."[42]

In research conducted for another doctoral dissertation in 1987, Christopher F. White contacted 425 cable subscribers in Austin, Texas, and interviewed

Table 3.3
Studies of Awareness of Public Access Television

Location	Year	Number of Respondents	Percent Aware of Public Access	Percent Who Watch
New York City	1973	250	30	30*
Columbus, IN	1974	643	N/A	2*
Manhattan, NY	1978	400+	50+	33**
Longmeadow, MA	1983	428	94	45**
Milwaukee, WI	1986	226	51	36*
Raleigh, NC	1988	400	76	58*
Sacramento, CA	1991	408	67	67*

*watch occasionally **watch regularly

Source: Linda K. Fuller, *Community Television in the United States*, Westport, CT: Greenwood Press, 1994, 12–15; and David Atkin and Robert LaRose, "Cable Access: Market Concerns Amidst the Marketplace of Ideas," *Journalism Quarterly* 68 (Fall 1991): 356–58.

Table 3.4
Comparison of Viewership among Cable Channels, 1986

CNN	*WTBS*	*ESPN*	*A&E*	*CBN*	*Lifetime*	*PUBLIC ACCESS*	*BET*	*C-SPAN*	*FNN*	*SPN*	*PTL*
61%	58%	47%	26%	21%	20%	14%	13%	12%	10%	8%	8 %

Source: David Atkin and Robert LaRose.

them regarding their viewing habits. Of the polled subscribers, 43 percent said that they had watched some programming on public access, although viewing was generally light. Not surprisingly, viewers of public access were also frequent viewers of programming on PBS and A&E. More significantly in terms of the mission of public access, White also found that subscribers who viewed public access exhibited higher levels of community involvement than those who did not.[43]

Survey results published in 1990 by the National Clearinghouse for Community Cable Viewership Research at Western Michigan University indicate that thirty million homes have public access channels on their cable system. This translates into approximately seventy million viewers, of whom almost 75 percent are aware of the public access channels.[44]

There is also anecdotal evidence which suggests that the impact of public access is growing steadily. In the small community of Cape May County, New Jersey, a half-hour special program on school overcrowding was repeated three times daily for two weeks leading up to a $1.1 million bond referendum. Producer Lenora Boninfante credited the program for both a huge turnout (more than 55 percent of voters cast ballots) and the passage of the referendum by a two to one margin.[45] Numerous candidates across the country have cited public access as a factor in increasing name recognition, especially when fighting a better-known and better-funded incumbent.

According to the Atkin and LaRose study, although the people who watch public access television are among the better educated, "heavy access viewers are nevertheless likely to be older, retired, and have lower incomes." The study goes on to say that "[a]ccording to the criterion for rating success among cable services, where a rating of 2 to 4 percent is considered strong, access channels nevertheless seem to be able to hold their own against the competition. Judging purely on the basis of audience viewership and satisfaction, it would seem that community channels have earned a place on the cable roster. That these channels can outperform more lavishly produced basic services should also establish their market value to cable operators."[46]

CONCLUSION

Local advocates deserve most of the credit for any public access television success. According to Chris Hill, an independent public access television producer,

"If there's good public access, it's a result of grassroots organizing by people who see this as an important public resource."[47] It would seem, then, that public access television is positioned for continued growth. The primary responsibility for assuring the availability and quality of public access television rests not with the Congress or the courts, but with the local citizenry whom it is intended to serve.

The battles for the future of public access television will be waged one by one, citizen by citizen, and community by community. Each municipality will have to determine for itself the value it places on the creation and support of a local, noncommercial television outlet. It is a battle most often waged on two fronts: philosophic and economic. If a community and its leaders are not convinced of the benefits of providing citizens with the means of producing their own television programs, the concept is unlikely to get off the ground. But even when advocates are able to muster political support, financial support is required for public access to survive and thrive. Although public access television organizations are funded primarily by the cable companies, local governments, and/or an educational institution, often funding is not at a sustainable level. Because of this insufficient funding, many public access television organizations are challenged to find additional sources of income.

NOTES

1. Bert Briller, "Accent on Access Television," *Television Quarterly* 28, no. 2 (Spring 1996): 51.

2. Anita Sharpe, "Television (A Special Report): What We Watch—Borrowed Time—Public-Access Stations Have a Problem: Cable Companies Don't Want Them Anymore," *Wall Street Journal*, 9 September 1994, sec. R, p. 12; Ralph Engelman, *Public Radio and Television in America: A Political History*, Thousand Oaks, CA: Sage, 1996, 257, 260. See also Pat Aufderheide, "Cable Television and the Public Interest," *Journal of Communication* 42 (Winter 1992): 58; *Public, Educational, and Government Access on Cable Television Fact Sheet*, Alliance for Community Media, Washington, DC.

3. *Community Media Resource Directory*, Washington, DC Alliance for Community Media, 1994, Appendices A–E; and *City of Greensboro Cable Task Force Report*, City of Greensboro, NC, September 1992. Unpublished.

4. James Barron, "Cable TV: The Big Picture," *New York Times*, 10 April 1994, p. 14.

5. Andy Newman, "More than Television," *New York Times*, 7 January 1996, New Jersey edition, p. 1.

6. Nancy Polk, "The View from New Haven; Public Access TV: It's Storer's Money, but Independent Talent," *New York Times*, 1 May 1994, sec. CN, p. 14; "Mission Viejo OKs Cable Channel for Public's Use," *Los Angeles Times*, 1 May 1993, Orange County edition, sec. B, p. 6; and Linda K. Fuller, *Community Television in the United States: A Sourcebook on Public, Educational, and Governmental Access,* (Westport, CT: Greenwood Press, 1994), 148.

7. See Chapter 4 for a more detailed analysis of public access funding.

8. Polk.

9. Fuller, 151; and Engelman, *Public Radio and Television in America*, 260.

10. Fuller, 149, 164–65.

11. Newman.

12. Beth Daley, "Tuning in Community TV," *Boston Sunday Globe*, 11 February 1996, North Weekly, p. 20; Fran Silverman, "News and Advice on TV for Haitians in the State," *New York Times*, 19 January 1992, Final edition, sec. CN, p. 12; Doyle Detroit, Westsound Community Access Television, Bremerton, Washington, <DDetroit@aol.com>, Alliance for Community Media Listserv (a national, on-line newsgroup for public access workers, supporters, and advocates), 29 March 1997, 1:06 PM; and Mohammad Karimi, *Iranian Television of Dallas: Cultural Issues, Preservation, and Community Formation*, Master's thesis, University of North Texas, 1997. Unpublished.

13. Tim Russell, Whitewater Community Television, Richmond, Indiana, <jarussel@indiana.edu>, Alliance for Community Media Listserv (a national, on-line news-group for public access workers, supporters, and advocates), 31 March 1997, 12:06 PM.

14. Jane Gross, "Using Cable TV to Get Child Support," New York Times, 14 November 1993, Final edition, sec. 1, p. 20.

15. Diane Ketcham, "Long Island Journal," *New York Times*, 23 September 1990, Final edition, sec. LI, p. 12.

16. John Kotarski, "Reporting Election Results Online," *The American City and County, Pittsfield* 113, no. 5 (May 1998): 8; Raymond Hernandez, "Albany on the Air: Politically Savvy and Cable-Ready," New York Times, 20 June 1996, sec. B, p. 1; and Theresa Young, "Public Access Reaching the Community through Cable TV," *FBI Law Enforcement Bulletin* 66, no. 6 (June 1997): 20–27.

17. Deborah Vinsel, "Community People, Community Access," *Community Media Review* 19, no. 4 (1996): 9, 12, 13.

18. Allan Johnson, "Television's Fringe Has its Say on Cable Access," *Chicago Tribune*, 6 December 1996, sec. 2, p. 1,6.

19. Johnson; Briller.

20. Briller.

21. Vinsel; Johnson.

22. Andrew Jacobs, "The Howard Stern of Cable," *New York Times*, 15 December 1996, p. 8CU; and Charles Gross, "Two on the Aisle: They're Public Access TV, Taking their Camcorder to Broadway Shows," *Camcorder* 13, no. 8 (August 1997): 94–98.

23. Ron Alexander and Ira Gallen, "Past Creates Wave of TV Nostalgia," *New York Times*, 2 August 1990, Final edition, sec. C, p. 1.

24. Susan Harris, "L.I. Cable Company Ordered to Restore a Public-Access Program," *New York Times*, 14 August 1994, Final edition, sec. 1, p. 44.

25. Jesse Katz, "New Episode of Tragedy Strikes a Mother's Crusade," *Los Angeles Times*, 4 April 1992, Home edition, sec. A, p. 1.

26. Bob Baker, "Poker Party's Freewheeling Ace," *Los Angeles Times*, 27 October 1992, Home edition, sec. F, p. 9.

27. Scott Harris, "They Watch their Television Religiously," *Los Angeles Times*, 2 May 1993, Valley edition, sec. B, p. 1.

28. Jim Washburn, "Crean's World; Spiders in the Salad! Towels Aflame! This is Cooking—on Local Cable, of Course," *Los Angeles Times*, 25 May 1993, Home edition, sec. E, p. 1; and Réne Chun, "Here's Joey!" *New York* 31, no. 18 (11 May 1998): 34.

29. Neil Strauss, "At 18, the 'Squirt TV' Guy Resumes his Pop-Scene Assault," *New York Times*, 9 September 1997, sec. C, p. 9; and Jim McConville, "MTV Makes 'Odd' Talk Choice," *Electronic Media* 16, no. 7 (10 February 1997): 8.

30. Patricia Aufderheide, "Underground Cable: A Survey of Public Access Programming," *Afterimage* (Summer 1994): 5–6.

31. James Maiella, Jr., "Marijuana Message on Public Access Cable TV Ignites Viewer's Outrage," *Los Angeles Times*, 13 November 1993, Home edition, sec. A, p. 28.

32. Barbara Dority, "Taking the Public Access out of Public Access," *The Humanist* 54, no. 6 (November 1994): 37; Aufderheide, "Underground Cable," 5–6; and Jane Smith, "The People's Channel," *Independent Weekly*, 16 November 1995, 21.

33. Fuller, 101.

34. Norman Vanamee, "Eat Drink Man Lizard," *New York* (11 November 1996): 20, 22.

35. "Public Access Cable Show Obscenity Convictions Upheld: Court 'Safe-Sex' Video not Educational," *News Media and the Law* 20, no. 1 (Winter 1996): 38; and W. Bernard Lukenbill, "Eroticized, AIDs-HIV Information on Public-Access Television: A Study of Obscenity, State Censorship and Cultural Resistance," *AIDS Education and Prevention* 10, no. 3 (1998): 230. The U.S. Supreme Court refused to hear the case; therefore the Appeals Court ruling stands.

36. Aufderheide, "Underground Cable," 5–6.

37. Mark D. Harmon, "Hate Groups and Cable Public Access," *Journal of Mass Media Ethics* 6, No. 3 (1991): 148–50.

38. Sharon B. Ingraham, "Access Channels: The Problem is Prejudice," *Multichannel News* 12, no. 37 (16 September 1991): 43; Aufderheide, "Underground Cable," 6.

39. Daley.

40. Linda K. Fuller, 12–15; and David Atkin and Robert LaRose, "Cable Access: Market Concerns Amidst the Marketplace of Ideas," *Journalism Quarterly* 68 (Fall 1991): 356–58.

41. Margaret B. Hardenbergh, "Promise versus Performance: A Case Study of Four Public Access Channels in Connecticut, (Ph.D. diss., New York University, 1985), 1.

42. Atkin and LaRose, 356–58.

43. Christopher F. White, "Eye on the Sparrow: Community Access Television in Austin, Texas," (Ph.D. diss., The University of Texas at Austin, 1988), 1.

44. Nicholson.

45. Newman, "More than Television," *New York Times*, 7 January 1996, New Jersey edition, p. 10.

46. Atkin and LaRose, 361.

47. Rick Szykowny, "The Threat of Public Access: An Interview with Chris Hill and Brian Springer," *The Humanist* 54 (1994): 23.

4

Current Funding Sources, Techniques, and Problems

Since its inception in the late 1960s, public access television has been funded through various means. The Junior Chamber of Commerce administered the first public access television center in Dale City, Virginia, with the channel provided by the cable company. As noted in Chapter 1, this public access television experiment ended due to lack of adequate funding and equipment. This common shortfall has had the effect of destabilizing the movement for public access television in many cities across the nation.

FUNDING SOURCES

The primary sources of funding for public access television generally include franchise fees, grants from the cable company, grants from the local government, or any combination of these. The method of funding is determined by the franchise agreement that the local government negotiates with the cable company. Private donations from individuals, foundations, and corporations generally comprise a very small part of the income for most public access television organizations.

Currently, there are 11,800 cable systems operating in 34,000 communities in the United States. Almost 65 million households subscribe to cable, which reaches an estimated 165 million people, or 65 percent of the television households in the United States. The 1984 Cable Communication Policy Act allows each local governmental entity to award a franchise agreement to the cable company providing service in its area. Section 541 of the Communications Act allows a franchise fee of up to 5 percent of the cable company's gross revenues to be paid to the local government as a fee for using the public rights-of-way to lay cable.[1]

Since the federal government began regulating cable television, franchise fees have had six basic rationales:

1. Revenue-raising—an opportunity to raise money for the local government without raising taxes.

2. Rent—rent for use of the public rights-of-way by the cable operator to lay cable.

3. Exclusivity—local municipalities help the cable company maintain a de facto monopoly on cable service.

4. Diversity—it is in the public interest to have public, educational, and governmental access to promote diversity.

5. Benefit—the cable company receives public relations benefits from having public, educational, and governmental access.

6. Regulatory—the cable company should pay for the costs the city incurs from having to regulate cable, for example, consultants, administrators, and inspectors.[2]

The rationale exercised most often for requiring a franchise fee is rent, although many public access television supporters believe that the diversity and benefit rationales are also valid. Few municipal administrators will admit that revenue-raising motivates them, but anecdotal evidence suggests that this is a significant factor in many cities.

Prior to 1984, local municipalities could assess a 3 percent franchise fee, and were allowed to assess an additional 2 percent if the additional monies were used to support public access television. The 1984 Cable Act raised the limit on the franchise fee to 5 percent, without stipulations. In many localities, the 5 percent franchise fee goes to the local government's general fund, with part of it going to fund public access television.[3]

Section 542(f) of the Communications Act also states: "A cable operator may designate that portion of a subscriber's bill attributable to the franchise fee as a separate item on the bill."[4] The key word in this section is "may"; cable companies are not required, but they "may." In many communities, this becomes a point of contention. Most cable companies list the franchise fee on cable bills so every cable subscriber will see this line item every time they pay their cable bill. The local government authority usually does not want this listed as a separate item. How franchise fees are characterized and billed can have a profound effect on attitudes toward public access television. Itemizing the franchise fee on the cable bill tends to make customers think of it as a tax. Omission of this separate line item draws less attention, puts the franchise fee in a general pool with all other cable services, and is more likely to be perceived as a fee-for-service rather than a tax. Since taxes are anathema to many voters, this distinction, even if it is only a perception, is important.

The cable company sees the franchise fee as an additional cost of doing business that the company is simply passing along to the subscriber. Conversely, local governments generally consider the franchise fee as a normal cost of doing business for the cable company. For public access television organizations, the monies generated from these fees, and how they are perceived by the public, can mean the difference between being funded, underfunded, or not funded at all.

Another source of funding for a public access television organization is a grant from the cable company. In these situations, the entire franchise fee goes directly into the local government's general fund and the cable company pays an additional sum to the public access television organization for operating and capital expenses. These grants are a negotiated part of the franchise agreement and are either paid directly to the public access television center or are paid to the local government, which then disperses the monies to the public access television center, usually on a quarterly basis.[5]

A third source of funding for public access television is the local government. If the local governmental entity operates the public access television center, the capital and operating budgets for public access television are a part of the capital and operating budgets of the local government. In other instances, a private, nonprofit organization operates public access television with the municipality providing funding. There are also cases in which a nonprofit organization operates public access television, but it is primarily supported by the cable company, with supplementary grants provided by the local government. It is rare that a local government will assume the entire burden of underwriting public access television operations.[6]

No matter what method of funding the public access television center uses in a locality, underfunding continues to be chronic for most centers. Different access centers have used different approaches to try to cover overhead costs and address long-term funding needs. The lion's share of costs for most public access television centers are for personnel (outreach, training, and administration) and equipment (purchase, maintenance, and replacement).

FUNDRAISING CHALLENGES FACED BY PUBLIC ACCESS TELEVISION

Public access television faces certain unique challenges in regard to fund raising. Public access comes under the classification of a social change or social movement organization, which attracts less than 5 percent of individual contributions and only 1 percent of the donations made by foundations. Compared to social service, health, or environmental advocates, public access television proponents have a more complicated, esoteric story to tell. Where other organizations can utilize real-life images of poverty, disease, or endangered animals to help their cause, the appeal of public access relies on the evocation of abstract ideas such as freedom of speech, community, democracy, and justice.[7]

Public access television does not readily elicit the kind of emotional reaction that motivates most people to give money. There are no heartwarming issues to advertise with public access and no impending crisis to make it a critical issue. Although the a crisis created by the increasing concentration of corporate ownership and control of the media makes a compelling argument, the mainstream press seldom advances this view. Consequently, the majority of Americans do not yet perceive this situation as a real threat to their well-being. To raise funds successfully, public access organizations must articulate a distinct vision and philosophy and then find an audience that shares this view. In this respect, public access organizations are like Public Citizen or People for the American Way on the left, and the Christian Coalition or the Moral Majority on the right.[8]

This is why, in terms of fund raising, public access television comes under the category of social change or social movement organizations.[9] These types of organizations seek to identify overarching problems within society and offer their services as a means of addressing these ills. The motivation for giving in these cases is comparatively subtle. The benefits are less tangible and more long term than for the Red Cross or the United Way. Donors must feel strongly about the concepts of freedom of speech, local control, media literacy, and public participation in the democratic process. The assumption is that people who give to these causes share a commitment to social change.

In addition to relying on abstract concepts and delayed gratification, public access television faces two more obstacles in the fund raising arena. First is the commitment of public access to its mission of being open to all voices within the community—the double-edged sword of openness. Except for broad federal or local standards of obscenity or indecency, public access operators are not permitted to exert undue influence on the messages and images that go out over their channels. Like the American Civil Liberties Union (ACLU), an organization that faces many of the same fund raising obstacles, public access often falls victim to its own principles. For example, the ACLU has periodically lost support from Jewish groups because it has defended the free speech rights of neo-Nazis. Similarly, public access often suffers in the public mind due to the unsavory, disrespectful, or offensive nature of a few of the programs it airs.

A second obstacle is that within the field of communications and broadcasting market forces are generally regarded to be meeting the demand for television programming, and the competition for profit is seen as being sufficient to attract the advertising revenues necessary to produce a variety of forms of speech and entertainment. When people think of social needs, they rarely think of the media as a place where their dollars are needed. The counterexamples to this rule are public radio and television, which provide the best models for public access television fund raising.

In the past, public radio and television enjoyed considerable government support, but both have incurred serious cutbacks in public sector funding and have had to become increasingly reliant on revenues from private sources, both individual and corporate. Public radio and television are probably the primary competitors for dollars that might otherwise go to public access television. Whatever the competition, however, these media outlets share a great advantage not enjoyed by most other nonprofits: they have direct access to the public via radio and television. In a nation of avid media consumers, television is the single most powerful tool for influencing public opinion and behavior.

But even with electronic access to the living rooms of cable subscribers, fund raising remains an uphill struggle for most public access centers. In fact, if it were not for the franchise fees and negotiated grants from cable companies built into the franchise agreements between municipalities and cable companies, many public access centers could not survive. Public access advocates must still get out into the communities they serve and compete with other nonprofit groups for financial support. Success in this endeavor will be determined by their ability to reach various segments of the community and demonstrate how public access serves their interests.

SOURCES OF FUND RAISING MONIES FOR PUBLIC ACCESS TELEVISION

A chart representing the various sources of funds, methods of fund raising, and types of gifts available to public access television is shown in Table 4.1. For most nonprofit organizations, roughly 90 percent of fund raising monies comes from individuals. The long-term success of some public access television operations often requires a significant amount of private donations; in others, the franchise fee is the sole source of financial support.[10]

The objectives of public access television are creating community, empowering people, encouraging public discourse, and promoting social change. By focusing on individuals in their fund raising activities, public access television centers will also be working toward their objectives. Fund raising can be used to help achieve the objectives of public access television not only through monetary support, but also through the fund raising process itself. By enlisting people's help in the fund raising effort, community will be created and public discourse will be inspired. By encouraging people to donate their time and money, people will be empowered and a climate conducive to social change will be promoted.[11]

Fund raising methods include annual and capital campaigns, planned giving, earned income, combined funds, in-kind donations, underwriting, special events, and foundation grantwriting. These methods can be used to acquire funds of various types, from basic membership fees to major gifts and endowments.

Two types of earned income are particularly suited to public access television and deserve special note. The first is underwriting, a type of funding in which individuals, groups, and corporations sponsor programs on public access television. In exchange for money to support a specific show or time period, the corporation will receive an on-air credit at the beginning or end of the show or several announcements during the time period. This type of funding is used frequently by public radio and television and is just beginning to be utilized by public access television organizations. The second is memberships, an important part of any public access television center's fund raising efforts. By encouraging or requiring anyone using the organization's facilities and equipment to become a

Table 4.1
Fund Raising Sources for Public Access Television Organizations

SOURCE	METHOD	TYPE
Individuals	Annual	New membership Membership renewal Member rejoining Additional gift Upgraded gift
	Capital	Major gift Assets
	Planned giving	Bequests Pooled income fund Charitable remainder trust
	Earned income	Special events Gaming Merchandising
	In-kind	Auction items Volunteer services
Corporations	Underwriting	Programs Paid PSAs Program fund Run-of-schedule
	Events	Sponsor Participant
	Grants	Parent organization grant Corporate membership Challenge grant Project funder Employee matching gifts
	In-kind	Premiums/auction items Management services Equipment/supplies Advertising space
	Earned income	Production services Joint ventures
Foundations	Unrestricted	General support
	Restricted	Specific projects
Governments	Federal State Local	Direct agencies: NTIA, NEA, NEH

Source: Alliance for Community Media, Washington, DC.

member, not only are funds raised, but as members, people become "stakeholders." A stakeholder is anyone who accepts and believes in the mission of the organization and commits to contribute to its cause. Public access television centers need to turn everyone who comes in contact with their organization into a stakeholder. And the way to do that is to introduce them to public access television, educate them, persuade them to become actively involved as members and producers, and then persuade them to give . . . and keep giving.[12]

For public access television organizations beginning to think about fund raising, the various methods must be assessed based on the organization's current resources. The criteria for judging possible fund raising methods include how much time the method will require, how many people will be needed, how much it will cost, and how much money it is expected to bring in. Questions typically asked include the following: Is there any special knowledge that may be needed? Will the funds received obligate the organization in some way? Is the funding source stable? What is the worst that could happen? What is the best that could be attained? Fund raising coordinators should answer each of these questions honestly to ascertain if the selected method is right for their organization.[13]

FUND RAISING SURVEY

To supplement the literature and help ascertain what techniques are being employed by public access television centers to contend with and manage this funding problem, surveys were mailed to 999 public, educational, and governmental (PEG) access centers in the United States.[14] (See Appendix 1 for a copy of the questionnaire and cover letter.) The three-page survey was mailed to all the PEG access centers listed in the most recent (1994) edition of the Alliance for Community Media *Community Media Resource Directory* (CMRD). In addition, the survey was posted on the Alliance for Community Media Listserv.[15]

The survey was designed to elicit information about the types of fund raising activities public access television centers are performing and included the following questions:

1. Please describe your most successful fund raising activities.
2. Please list any other income-generating activities.
3. What is your approximate annual budget?
4. From what sources is your center funded *and* what percentage of your annual budget comes from each source?
5. In what ways have funding sources impacted your programming? Are there any noticeable changes in programming in the last few years and have any of these resulted in a change of fund raising?
6. What problems, if any, have you faced with fund raising and funding?
7. What types of programming do you cablecast and what percentage of your total programming does each type comprise?
8. How many subscribers does your cable system currently have?

9. How many active producers does your center have?

10. How many hours do you cablecast each week? How many hours are produced locally?

11. How do you generate viewers and producers?

12. Is there anything I did not raise above you would like to share with me?

The questions were deliberately posed in an open-ended manner to avoid assumptions, remove any limitations upon the respondents, and to allow respondents to disclose all possible responses to each question without leading or prompting.[16]

With fifty useable responses (and six returns for incorrect addresses), the response rate was 5 percent. Although the response rate was small, the information gleaned provides a valuable first approximation into the fund raising practices of public access television centers. As the following analysis and discussion will show, planned fund raising for public access television is beginning to take hold with a variety of ideas being implemented, although there are a few administrators who think fund raising is unnecessary. Based on survey responses and anecdotal evidence, it seems clear that the administrators who are not motivated to undertake supplementary fund raising activities are those whose revenue needs are met through franchise agreements or whose services are nominal. (See Appendix 1 for the survey's raw data.)

FUND RAISING ACTIVITIES

Because of the open-ended nature of the questions, it was necessary to code and group responses to each question. Items 1 and 2—"Please describe your most successful fund raising activities" and "Please list any other income-generating activities"—were combined, as the responses to both were interchangeable for purposes of this research. From items 1 and 2, it could be determined not only what types of fund raising public access television organizations were doing but also whether they were fund raising at all. Of the fifty respondents, twenty-four were doing some type of fund raising. A list of the types of fund raising being conducted by public access television centers is shown in Table 4.2.

Public access television centers reported the acquisition of earned income in several different ways. Earned income includes monies received from any goods or services that are sold. The primary method is through membership fees. Most public access television centers require anyone wanting to use the facility or equipment to become a member of the organization. For example, in Greensboro, North Carolina, the membership fee is $35 per year for individuals; $50 for non-profit organizations; and $200 for for-profit businesses. Individuals and nonprofit organizations can have their membership dues waived in lieu of volunteer service to Greensboro Community Television. Another earned income strategy is to charge for workshops and classes. To use the facility or equipment, a person must either demonstrate proficiency with the equipment or attend a class and pass a

Table 4.2
Types of Public Access Television Fund Raising and the Percentage of Respondents Conducting Each Type

Type of Fund Raising	Percent
Earned income	34
Donations	34
Events	26
Underwriting	22
Grants	6
Capital campaigns	2

test. In some cases, volunteer time can also be substituted for class and workshop fees for individuals and nonprofit organizations. Many public access television centers also sell new videotapes as a convenience for their users in addition to charging for dubbing videotapes. A few public access television centers agree to videotape certain events that have broad appeal so they will be able to sell copies of the tapes. These events include sports, graduations, musical concerts, proms, high school senior memory videos, and parades, among others. One center was able to get a copy of a 1953 film about their town and sell copies of it; another produces biographies for local citizens for a donation. Two public access television centers offered to produce programs for individuals and organizations on a fee basis. A few centers sell ads in their newsletters. Several centers provide Internet access. One center videotapes holiday messages (video greeting cards) in their studio upon request and asks for a small donation for each. The greetings are edited together and played twenty-four hours a day for a week leading up to the holiday. In a less common situation, one public access television center charged producers a $20 enrollment fee and $52 per year to use the facility. Another charged users for studio and editing time.[17] More commonly, only nonmembers are charged for equipment and facility use. Most centers also sell T-shirts, mugs, bumper stickers, and other promotional items. One center reported that they sold their old equipment to raise money. During a local music festival, a public access television center supplied volunteers to sell concessions and the festival sponsors donated part of the proceeds from the concession sales to the center.

Another primary means of fund raising for public access television centers is through private donations. Methods of acquiring donations include asking local businesses, organizations, social service agencies, and churches for general donations or support on specific projects; receiving the proceeds from "parking day" at the local municipal parking garage; a major donor campaign; a check-off campaign on the cable bill where subscribers can donate a dollar every month; in-kind donations from businesses of backdrops, flower arrangements, tapes, and other items, including door prizes for an event; United Way Donor Option Campaigns; direct appeal to cable viewers via bill stuffers; on-channel solicitation; appeals from producers to friends and relatives to help with production costs; and approaching local restaurants to donate food for production volunteers.

Another means of fund raising is to sponsor an event. Public access television centers have generally found these to be less successful at raising money than earned income or donations, and putting on an event often entails a great deal of effort. Events reported in the survey included an eight-hour telethon of live community talent; a walk-a-thon; a benefit performance at a local theatre; a tag sale; a celebrity reception; an on-air fund raiser; an on-air auction; a concert series; a senior citizens ball with a sixteen-piece orchestra; tournaments including boys' and girls' basketball, wrestling, softball, and miniature golf; an awards event; a tenth anniversary party; an annual large telethon in partnership with another non-profit organization for twenty-six hours that included an auction and entertainment; and a phonathon in which every citizen in a town of three thousand was called and asked to have $1 added to their cable bill to support public access television, which resulted in $14,000 for one year!

The respondent who reported conducting an awards event and a tenth anniversary party noted that both events ended up costing them money. Some events were scheduled annually, while some were conducted once. One respondent commented that the events they had conducted (tag sales, celebrity reception, and tennis tournaments) had all been "a lot of work and some fun, but none have been as lucrative as the phone calls."

Underwriting is a form of sponsorship in which an organization provides financial support to a specific show. In some cases, the public access television center recruits sponsors for special programs, but generally it falls to the producer of a specific show to recruit sponsors. In return for their support, the sponsor's name is mentioned on the show. Many public access television centers use policies developed in recent years by PBS to help formulate their own policies regarding underwriting. In addition, several respondents reported underwriting (or sponsorship) of shows in the form of a sponsor fee, and also sponsorship of the community bulletin board. Underwriting is solicited from individuals, organizations, and businesses.

Only a few centers reported grants as a type of fund raising. In one instance, producers applied for grants using the public access television organization as the necessary nonprofit conduit. In this case, the public access television organization received a 10 percent conduit fee. The same organization also received a direct $24,000 grant to produce a series of four live, educational programs.

Only one public access television organization reported conducting a capital campaign. That center was able to raise $1.2 million dollars for a new building. This center has had phenomenal success at fund raising, primarily because of the center's dynamic executive director and his relationships within the community.

IMPACT OF FUND RAISING

In response to item 5, "In what ways have funding sources impacted your programming? Are there any noticeable changes in programming in the last few years and have any of these resulted in a change of fund raising?" respondents indicated that fund raising had little impact on programming. Responses fell into six categories: more funding equals better programming; more funding equals better equipment; generally negative; political interference from local elected officials; increased stress on personnel; no impact; and generally positive. (See Table 4.3.)

Overall, remarks about the impact of fund raising on programming were positive and specific. The one nonspecific positive comment said that as the number of cable subscribers increased, their funds increased and this had a positive effect on their budget. Other positive comments indicated that increases in funding resulted in better equipment and better programming. As one might expect, access operators reported that they were able to do more with more money. One respondent stated: "Funding has allowed us to make great improvements in quality of equipment and set pieces used to produce programming. The noticeable changes are increased programming, more efficient use of facilities, better quality video and editing, better audio, improved station signal, live programming capability, the ability to receive satellite transmissions, and increased numbers of programs." This was the overall tone of most of the positive comments. Negative comments used the same argument in terms of shortfall, that is, less funding translates into less equipment and less and poorer quality programming. As one respondent put it: "If you have minimal funding, you cannot purchase the electronic equipment you need. Usually it becomes piecemeal, a little of this, this year, a little of that, the next year. So quality, or similar look that the local stations have, does not happen. The equipment needs to be maintained."

Negative comments also included difficulties with local elected officials. Because most public access television centers receive funding via the franchise

Table 4.3
Impact of Fund Raising on Public Access Television and the Percentage of Respondents Reporting Each Type

Type of Impact	Percent
More funding/better programming	18
More funding/better equipment	8
Negative (general)	8
Political interference	6
Stress on personnel	4
No impact	4
Positive (general)	2

agreement the local municipality has with the cable company, local officials sometimes get involved in funding decisions. Even if the amount is specified in the franchise agreement, public access television staff tend to be sensitized to local politics because the contract is renewed approximately every ten years. One respondent noted that there was occasional political interference and another noted that the city wanted to cut back funding so there would be more money for the city's general fund without raising taxes. As one respondent stated: "Being on the purse strings of the government means we need to take into account their wishes over the general public's requests." And it is not only the access center's staff that has to be conscious of this dependent relationship with the local government. Another respondent stated: "We do have one ultra-conservative producer who managed to ire [sic] a banker on the City Council, but that is just a small part of our problems with the City Council."

Two respondents mentioned the impact fund raising has on their staff. These comments were generally negative. Generally, the number of staff varies from center to center depending upon the size of the center's budget, and usually ranges from five to ten, but can be as little as one and as many as twenty-five. Most staff have little time for fund raising, and yet frequently without fund raising there is not enough money to pay salaries. If the staff focuses on fund raising, there is less time for training and outreach.

Comments about the impact of fund raising on programming tended to be positive if the respondent felt she had enough money and negative if the respondent felt she did not have enough money. Most people declined to offer specifics, focusing instead on the more general impacts of funding.

FUND RAISING PROBLEMS

The fund raising issues that surfaced in the survey can be placed into five categories—four problem areas and a no-problem area. The four problem areas are competition for gift dollars, convincing elected officials to fund public access television, lack of time or staff to raise funds, and the difficulty of selling public access television as a worthy cause. (See Table 4.4.)

Table 4.4
Fund Raising Problems in Public Access Television and the Percentage of Respondents Reporting Each

Problem	Percent
Difficulty selling public access television to donors	18
Not enough time/staff	14
Competition for gift dollars	6
Difficulty convincing elected officials	2
No problem	18

The most prevalent problem identified in the survey was difficulty in selling public access television as a worthy cause to prospective donors, a problem faced by most nonprofit organizations. It is especially difficult for public access television because, as one respondent put it: "Some feel franchise fees should be enough." Or as another respondent stated, "We have experienced an attitude from foundations and corporations that public access television is a luxury and since we're not feeding the hungry or taking care of the homeless, money doesn't flow freely." Other responses with a similar tone included "[We have difficulty] establishing a clear public image of what we are, what we do, and what we are not," and "We are a fiscally sound organization with guaranteed payments from the cable franchise. Funders look for 'poorer' organizations to fund. We are also a technical assistance provider and media. Two more strikes against us in the funding arena." Another respondent said that "the 'bake sale' approach to fund raising is simply not very productive—very small returns for a lot of work." Perhaps the most eloquent response was this: "Raising dollars is an art form. We are still in the infancy stage. We have a problem fitting into the square pegs criteria for funding. We fall through the cracks. We are a public, governmental and educational access, bona fide 501(c)(3) nonprofit. We have letters of rejections, no answer, or do not qualify. Fund raising is a long, slow, arduous journey we have no expertise in." One respondent said that the only problem she had was convincing the borough council to increase funding due to rising costs.

Staff and time limitations also are seen as problems when public access television organizations try to do fund raising. Most public access television centers have a limited staff and with fewer people there is little time to raise funds. In fact, several people responded that they did no fund raising because of a lack of time. Volunteers could be used for help with fund raising, but, as one respondent stated, most public access television volunteers are generally attracted by production opportunities. Unlike many social service organizations, in which volunteers are accustomed to being assigned administrative tasks, most of those who volunteer to work at a public access television center expect to take part in making television programs.

Not only are public access television centers faced with trying to convince people of the value of public access television with limited time and staff, there is also a sense that there is more competition for gift dollars. Several respondents mentioned competition for dollars and tightening budgets. "Money is tight, especially in a small, rural county like ours. We consider it a problem that only people who have money—or who find paying sponsors—can expect to get productions made." Or as another respondent put it: "Obviously, recessions are never good for nonprofits. We barely survived the early 1990s. The station is in an area that is saturated with nonprofits and competition for dollars is keen."

Some of the respondents reported they did not have any problems with fund raising, but this was primarily because they were not doing any fund raising. The remaining few seemed optimistic, or at least philosophical, about fund raising.

One stated: "The public does not mind an increase because they understand the value," and "We have had to seek additional funding since our inception."

The four primary problem areas related to fund raising illuminated by this survey—competition for gift dollars, convincing elected officials to fund public access television, lack of time and staff to raise funds, and the difficulty of selling public access television as a worthy cause—are common to almost all nonprofits. Only in having to win over basic public approval of the enterprise do public access television centers have a demonstrably more difficult task than other nonprofit groups.[18]

TYPES OF PROGRAMMING

Respondents reported an extremely wide range of types of programming. The categories of programming distilled from the variety of responses were informational, entertainment, religious, sports, arts, children's, miscellaneous, public, educational, and governmental. (See Table 4.5.) Responses ranged from "public, educational, governmental, and children's" to "100 percent community programming" to "Our programming has complete variety. We are public, educational, and governmental. I am required by law to program just about anything." Many respondents listed all their program types, and the percentage of total programming for each. For example, "Talk, 30 percent; religious, 25 percent; town meetings, 15 percent; town events, 15 percent; sports, 5 percent; entertainment and miscellaneous, 10 percent" and "Religious, 15 percent; political viewpoint, 20 percent; senior issues, 2 percent; gay, 2 percent; other languages, 4 percent; health, 10 percent; entertainment, 30 percent; miscellaneous (cooking, travel, special interests), 17 percent." The wide variety of responses and the mutual inexclusivity of the categories made analysis of the data difficult.

Table 4.5
Types of Public Access Television Programming and the Percentage of Respondents Reporting Each Type (Note: Categories Overlap)

Types of Programming	Percent
Informational	26
Entertainment	13
Religious	17
Sports	13
Arts	5
Children's	3
Miscellaneous	12
Public	12
Educational	14
Governmental	20

ADDITIONAL DATA

The survey contained several questions only peripherally related to fund raising, such as number of subscribers and producers; hours cablecast; hours produced locally; how the center generates viewers and producers; and other items. These questions were included to help get a general picture of the respondents and their PEG centers.

The number of subscribers and producers was as varied as the programming. The number of cable subscribers served by each public access television organization ranged from 1,500 to 500,000. The number of producers ranged from zero to two thousand, although in some cases it was unclear whether the number reported reflected the number of active producers or just members of the organization. One respondent reported seven hundred "certified users," although the question asked for number of "active producers." A certified user is one who is adequately trained to use center equipment, but this does not mean all these users are active. For this particular center, active producers may actually be certified users, but the response remains unclear.

Hours cablecast each week, as reported on the survey, ranged from zero to 576 hours. The percentage of total hours cablecast of locally produced programs ranged from zero to 100 percent. Because of the openness of the questions, it is uncertain how much of the programming counted was actually locally produced, or whether the community bulletin board was also included in the total. If the respondent counted the community bulletin board as local programming, then it is conceivable that a center could be cablecasting locally produced programming twenty-four hours per day. Analysis of the raw data showed almost one-third of the respondents reported that locally produced programming comprised 50 to 85 percent of their total hours cablecast.

Public access television centers are generating viewers and producers in a number of ways. These tactics can be grouped into eight similar categories: press coverage, promos on the channel, word-of-mouth, cross media promotions, quality programming on the channel, newsletter, speaker's bureau, listing on the Prevue Channel, ad in cable guide, or other. (See Table 4.6.)

Most respondents listed more than one tactic for generating viewers and producers. Press coverage was reported by twenty respondents as being a good way to get the word out. As one respondent put it, "Viewers are generated through press releases in the local papers. We find that if they watch one show, they usually stay around for the next show. Many of our producers have approached us— we find that we rarely need to recruit producers. Word-of-mouth is also very strong in the community." Another response was "Heavy PR in local newspapers, promos on our channel."

The Prevue Channel is a cable channel that continuously shows what is being aired on all the channels on that cable system for the current hour and a half. In many locations, public access television is listed only as "public access programming," and specific shows are not listed. However, a few public access television

Table 4.6
How Public Access Television Centers Generate Viewers and Producers, and the Percentage of Respondents Reporting Each Method

Generating Viewers & Producers	Percent
Press coverage	20
Promos on the channel	18
Word-of-mouth	14
Cross media promotions	8
Good programming on the channel	7
Newsletter	4
Speaker's bureau	3
Prevue Guide listing	2
Cable Guide ad	1
Other	18

centers have discovered they can get their shows listed on the Prevue Channel for a monthly fee of $50.

Another problem encountered by some public access television centers is the reluctance of some local newspapers to list public access television shows in their weekly television guides. Some of this disinclination may be because the public access channel's schedules change frequently, and many newspaper television schedules are published a few weeks in advance by newspaper syndicates. There is anecdotal evidence that suggests, however, that a negative attitude exists at some local newspapers toward public access television; since cable access represents a certain level of competition for the print media, such adversarial feelings are hardly surprising. Several respondents reported that their local newspapers had agreed to print the public access television program schedule in another section of the newspaper each week. For example, in Greensboro, North Carolina, the public, educational, and governmental access weekly schedules are printed in the "People and Places" section that appears every Sunday.

Responses that fell into the "Other" category included sending out program flyers, open houses, training workshops, taping community events, putting on a telethon, advertising in schools, posting notices in libraries and community centers, and conducting a viewership survey.

OTHER COMMENTS

Question 12 asked if the respondents had anything else they wanted to say that had not been covered by the other questions. This question elicited a variety of comments. A few of them dealt with fund raising and some were about public access television in general, while others were personal to the respondent's experience. A selection of these responses follows. (See Appendix 1 for a complete listing of responses to all the questions.)

In a rural area serving seventeen little towns over seventy miles. Cable company is cooperatively owned, has no real profits to share with us and no franchise agreements.

We are exploring changing the focus [from] 80 to 90 percent for the independent producer and 10 to 20 percent for the nonprofit organization to 80 to 90 percent for the nonprofit and 10 to 20 percent for the independent producer. The change is due to the low usage, low viewers, and the need to do more for the nonprofit community in promoting their services.

Since cable revenues have declined over the last few years, public access centers need to find a way to increase the number of sources for revenue. We have had success working with other nonprofits on joint grants. They provide much publicity for both organizations. Grantors like to fund these projects.

We try to make ourselves invaluable to the community in order to insure future funding through grants and fees. We do not rely on fund raising, because it takes away time from working with our producers.

With the exception of extremists, such as hate groups or naked talk shows from California and New York, most all public access shows are decent and sincere, and they are the only places on earth where the average person can access mass media without censorship.

We figure our initial growth and our continued development is tied to this god called money. Our growth was slowed considerably and some staff were overburdened with trying to meet the public's need for offering reasonable services. If one machine breaks down or needs repair we experience delays and in some cases monetary shortfalls. However, all is not despair, we do manage to function well and increase the volunteer and viewer base. (fundage sucks!)

We are a small group of volunteers who named ourselves C.A.C.T.US a year ago so we could get a better identity. It's Concord Area Community TV is US. Grammar is incorrect, but CACTWE just sounded too strange. We think access can be of great benefit to a community. We come together with different philosophies and visions and have supported each other because we see real value in access plus it gives an opportunity for doing something we also enjoy. It's been a long struggle and it isn't over yet, but it's worth the effort.

When you start growing by leaps and bounds as we have the last four years, you run out of resources: Be careful what you pray for!

CONCLUSION

In an era when there has been a general movement toward privatization of functions that had previously been in the public or governmental domain, public access television is clearly bucking the trend. With public access television, citizens are being asked to support a media enterprise that has previously been operated exclusively by the private or governmental sector. The factor that should turn this battle in favor of public access television is that operational costs are generally provided through franchise agreements, and funds solicited directly from the public are usually supplemental. This means that communities are being offered a service for which they do not have to pay, except in the form of costs that may be passed along by local cable operators. This would seem to make public access television an "easy sell" to communities and to local officials, but such is rarely the case. Fund raising has been identified as a problem by most nonprofits, and this survey offers clear evidence that this problem is compounded in the field of public access cable television.

NOTES

1. *Broadcasting and Cable Yearbook 1998*, vol. 2 (New Providence, NJ: R. R. Bowker, 1998): xi; and *U.S. Code*, vol. 47, sec. 541–42.

2. David J. Saylor, "Municipal Ripoff: The Unconstitutionality of Cable Television Franchise Fees and Access Support Payments," *Catholic University Law Review* 35 (Spring 1986): 676–77.

3. Ibid., 686.

4. *U.S. Code*, vol. 47, sec. 542

5. Linda K. Fuller, *Community Television in the United States: A Sourcebook on Public, Educational, and Governmental Access*, (Westport, CT: Greenwood Press, 1994), 2; and Ralph Engelman, *Public Radio and Television in America: A Political History*, (Thousand Oaks, CA: Sage Publications, 1996), 260.

6. See, e.g., Davis Community TV, Santa Fe Public Access, DATV—Dayton Access Television, Redding Community Access Corp., and Mid-Peninsula Access Corporation, *Community Media Resource Directory*, (Washington, DC: Alliance for Community Media, 1994), 13, 27–28, 179, 184, 197. Perhaps the most important fund raising tool that nonprofit organizations have is their nonprofit certification, bestowed by the Internal Revenue Service (IRS). This certification allows donors to deduct contributions from their taxes. How much one can deduct depends upon the type of nonprofit organization (the IRS has several categories), the organization's tax bracket, and other variables.

7. In 1996, a total of $150.7 billion was given to nonprofit organizations in the United States. Of this figure, individuals gave 85.5 percent or $130 billion. (Ann Kaplan, ed., *Giving USA 1996, Annual Report on Philanthropy for the Year 1996*, [Norwalk, CT: AAFRC Trust for Philanthropy, 1997], 16–17.) The reasons people are so generous, according to Michael Seltzer, a pioneer in nonprofit management and fund raising, fall into six areas: to act on their values and beliefs, to help create and maintain a sense of community, to increase their sense of personal worth, to leave something for posterity, to have fun and create pleasure, and to feel good. Typical sources of funding include individuals, corporations, foundations, and government agencies. Although there is a tendency to think of foundations and corporations as being the biggest contributors to nonprofit groups, as mentioned earlier, almost 90 percent of the total private (nongovernment) dollars given to nonprofit organizations comes from individuals. Therefore, except for nonprofit agencies such as Head Start that are largely supported by government, most nonprofit fund raising efforts should be directed toward individual donors. (Susan A. Ostrander, *Money for Change: Social Movement Philanthropy at Haymarket People's Fund*, [Philadelphia: Temple University Press, 1995], 13–14; and Michael Seltzer, *Securing Your Organization's*

Future, [New York: The Foundation Center, 1987], 101, 104–105, 400. See also Ram Cnaan and Felice Perlmutter, "Using Private Money to Finance Public Services: The Case of the Philadelphia Department of Recreation," *New Directions for Philanthropic Fundraising*, [Fall 1995]: 53–73.)

8. In sales and telemarketing, since the goal is to get potential customers to part with their money for a product or service, the emphasis is generally on the art of how people are approached, and methods are based on principles of human psychology. One of the foremost rules in this process is not to take no for an answer. But in the nonprofit arena, tactics such as arm-twisting and aggressive manipulation are generally unproductive. For many nonprofits, a simple mailing (or series of mailings) is sufficient to get people to pull out their checkbooks. As Henry A. Rosso, founder and Director Emeritus of The Fund Raising School, a program of the Indiana University Center on Philanthropy, points out in his essay "The Philosophy of Fund Raising," it is the organization and the purpose for which it exists that give meaning to fund raising. Fund raising is the opportunity for the contributor to experience the satisfaction of supporting a worthwhile cause in which that person believes. (Henry A. Rosso, "The Philosophy of Fund Raising" in *Achieving Excellence in Fund Raising*, [San Francisco: Jossey-Bass], 1991, 9–11. See also Seltzer, 90–92.)

9. Kim Klein, author of *Fundraising for Social Change*, offers a broader view that acknowledges motives of self-interest. One of her three major principles of fund raising is that "[P]eople give money to charity because it serves their interest." (Klein's other two principles are that diversity of funding sources is the secret of financial stability and that anyone can learn to do fund raising.) Along similar lines, Fisher Howe, a leading fund raising researcher and practitioner, outlines six principles of philanthropic giving:

1. People give money because they want to.

2. People don't give unless they're asked (and people don't give large donations unless they are asked to consider large donations).

3. People give money to people.

4. People give money to opportunities, not to needs.

5. People give to success, not to distress.

6. People give money to make a change for good. And Robert L. Payton, et al., see the mission of philanthropy "as a tradition based on three very simple and powerful premises: 1) things go wrong, 2) things could always be better, and 3) voluntary initiatives are often appropriate responses to either or both of the first two."

(Kim Klein, *Fund Raising for Social Change*, [Inverness, CA: Chardon Press], 1988, 16–17; Fisher Howe, *The Board Member's Guide to Fund Raising* [San Francisco: Jossey-Bass, 1991], 6–8; and Robert L. Payton, Henry A. Rosso, and Eugene R. Tempel, "Toward a Philosophy of Fund Raising" in *Taking Fund Raising Seriously*, ed. Dwight F. Burlingame and Lamont J. Hulse, [San Francisco: Jossey-Bass, 1991], 6.)

10. Ann Kaplan, ed., *Giving USA 1996, Annual Report on Philanthropy for the Year 1996*, (Norwalk, CT: AAFRC Trust for Philanthropy, 1997), 16–17. See also Seltzer, 4, 65–67.

11. For many nonprofits, fund raising is viewed as a necessary evil. This is due in large measure to a general lack of fund raising experience. To offset this negative perception, two ideas must be communicated. First, properly executed, fund raising is not an adjunct

to the work of the organization, but integral to it. It is not an isolated function, but part of the overall marketing and development of the organization. Second, fund raising is a process that can be learned.

12. Rosso, "A Philosophy of Fund Raising," 6–7.

13. Klein, 26. See also Seltzer, 399–456.

14. Funding of this survey was provided by the Eli A. and Minnie S. Rubinstein Scholarship Award of $600, received from the School of Journalism and Mass Communication at the University of North Carolina at Chapel Hill, April 1997.

15. A listserv is an e-mail-based interactive discussion forum on a particular topic to which e-mail users may subscribe. The listserv distributes all e-mail received by the list address to each subscriber on the list. Subscribers can post and receive messages to and from all the other subscribers. The Alliance for Community Media listserv is available to all ACM members.

16. Although the open-ended nature of the questions may have increased the diversity of the responses, hindsight leads the writer to believe that this type of question may also have discouraged people from responding, as they may have felt the survey would take too much time to complete. Additionally, the first sentence in the cover letter about the need for funds by public access television centers may also have prejudiced the results of this study.

17. This center reported that the fees have not deterred many people—they are breaking production records—and that the $10,000 to $12,000 earned makes up 20 to 25 percent of their annual budget.

18. One of the most basic things to remember about fund raising is that in order to get money the organization must ask for it. As Klein notes in *Fund Raising for Social Change*, the reasons religious organizations raise the most money from the private sector are because they ask regularly, they make it easy to give, and they offer many different kinds of programs for people to support. (Klein, 14–15. See also Wilson C. Lewis, "Investing More Money in Fund Raising—Wisely," in *Taking Fund Raising Seriously*, ed. Dwight F. Burlingame and Lamont J. Hulse, [San Francisco: Jossey-Bass, 1991], 258–59.)

5

The Future of Public Access Television

In the 1950s and 1960s, as television assumed a dominant role in American culture, commercial television was the only option. As Tony Schwartz states in *The Responsive Chord*, "When commercial television was the only form of programming available, the public accepted it as synonymous with television."[1] With the advent of public television (PBS and CPB) in the 1960s, the public began to be aware of alternatives to mainstream, commercial television. Viewers gradually became accustomed to the public television alternative, with its greater focus on quality and education, and relative absence of advertising. It entered the public consciousness that there was more than one television environment. As public television moved toward the mainstream in the 1970s, public access television became the new option. Public access television differed from public television less in content or form than in having been created by ordinary citizens. In recent years, of course, other television environments have become available (for example, pay-per-view and direct television satellite feeds). Public control of the means of production, however, remains the essential fact that distinguishes public access television from other forms of television. Public control is the primary attribute that must be emphasized if this media alternative is to survive and flourish. The overarching recommendation for any public access television operation, therefore, is to increase public participation in the process of making programs.

In seeking broad public participation, public access television faces certain unique obstacles. Unlike the situation with most civic or social service organizations, the basic concept of public access television itself is not always embraced by the general public. Not every citizen is actively involved with the Red Cross or Hospice, to name two well-known nonprofit organizations, but most have a general feeling of good will and appreciation toward these institutions. Public access television often lacks this kind of broad-based support.

There are several reasons for this softness of basic support. First, public access television is new to many communities, and people tend to be fearful or suspicious of what they do not know. The attitude toward public access television is often formed more by reputation than by firsthand experience. Due to the strict adherence of public access television organizations to First Amendment principles of openness, and the occasional controversies that inevitably follow, this reputation has often been mixed. To the extent people *have* heard about public access television, what they have heard is often negative.

A second factor that puts public access television at a disadvantage in the public eye is that most people regard the media as a specialized field dominated by professionals and closed to the average citizen. Even when given the opportunity, most people find it hard to believe that it is within their capability to produce a television program. In this instance, the attitude expressed is more likely to be indifference than negativity, but the effect on a public access television operation is much the same.

A third factor, which is more difficult to pinpoint, is the leftist political category in which many people tend to put public access television. Ever since the early, patently political pronouncements that promoted public access television as "guerrilla television," public access television advocates have generally taken pains to portray their service as neither left nor right, but open to all points of view. But this early association with so-called radical elements, combined with the inevitable fears that arise in each community about where all this "openness" might lead, has led to skepticism and suspicion in many communities toward public access television. This has resulted in the medium often being regarded less as an opportunity for participation in the "marketplace of ideas" than as a part of a larger movement for social change with which only a few citizens identify.

Kim Klein, in *Fundraising for Social Change*, could be talking about many public access television organizations when she states: "Many people will not agree with or even understand what your group is trying to do. Your organization probably has little immediate public recognition, and if you are seeking to change the status quo, people may feel threatened by your program. Even those in sympathy with what you are trying to accomplish may think that you are hopelessly naive or idealistic, and you will often be told to face reality."[2] To combat this perceived naiveté, public access television advocates can utilize the recommendations outlined in the remainder of this chapter to help secure the future of public access television.

THE SURVIVAL OF PUBLIC ACCESS TELEVISION

The relative newness of public access television in many communities, the perception of the media as being dominated by professionals and closed to the rest of us, and the view that public access television is a radical arena, mean that the survival of this valuable community resource is not assured. Based on the research, including the results of the survey discussed in Chapter 4, this section contains six general recommendations, offered to ensure the survival of the electronic soapbox into the twenty-first century.

First, a great deal of time and effort must be put into improving public understanding of public access television and increasing the participation of the local community in making programs. Without increased public awareness there will be little or no support, and without public participation there is little reason for such support to exist. The two main avenues available for public access television centers to increase awareness and participation are through the use of the cable television channels available to them, and through marketing and public relations.

The second recommendation is for public access television centers to map out a comprehensive fund raising plan, including the designation of a fund raising coordinator. It must be recognized, however, that although the ability to attract funds is essential, there is little chance that this task can be carried out successfully unless the groundwork is laid by creating a higher profile and a more positive image for public access television. Additionally, although it may seem self-evident, many nonprofit organizations fail precisely because no single individual accepts the responsibility for developing, implementing, and overseeing fund raising strategies. That is why the designation of a fund raising coordinator is as important as the creation of a fund raising plan.

The third recommendation is for public access television centers to become more proactive in creating and implementing media literacy programs at the national, state, and local levels. Such programs help to broaden the pool of citizens who understand how the media work. This larger group of media-literate people will be more likely to appreciate the importance of public access television.

The fourth recommendation is for advocates to join the Alliance for Community Media. This professional organization offers important information and support that is necessary for maintaining the capability and resolve of a public access television center and gives centers a voice in lobbying for regulatory reforms at the national level.

Fifth, it is recommended that public access television centers create and maintain a good relationship with their funding sources. Working with the local cable company, especially, can ultimately help proponents of the cable industry understand the importance and value of public access television to the community as well as to the cable industry's own economic well-being.

Table 5.1
Six Recommendations for Securing the Future of Public Access Television

1. Increase public awareness.
2. Create and implement a detailed fund raising plan.
3. Create and implement a media literacy plan.
4. Join the Alliance for Community Media.
5. Maintain a good relationship with funding organizations.
6. Work at every level to strengthen public access regulations.

Lastly, public access television advocates and supporters should work at the federal, state, and local levels to have regulations implemented to ensure the continued availability and future promotion of public access television. (See Table 5.1.)

RAISING AWARENESS AND INCREASING PARTICIPATION

There are many ways to go about getting a message across to the public, but public access television operators enjoy an obvious advantage over most other groups: they program a television channel. Not only does the channel afford multiple opportunities for self-promotion, such as bulletin boards, program notes, and public service announcements, it offers an inducement that is as basic and powerful as the human ego. People love to see themselves (and people they know) on television. Although one of the objectives of public access television is to demystify the process of making television, most people still regard it as a thrilling, almost magical force, and access advocates would be remiss if they did not capitalize on this power. The best way for public access television to ingratiate itself with the community it serves is to seize every opportunity to get as many citizens involved as possible, whether in front of or behind the camera. The general goal is to weave public access television into the fabric of community life so thoroughly that it becomes an indispensable part of the community's daily life. As one respondent put it, "We try to make ourselves invaluable to the community in order to insure future funding through grants and fees."

To the extent that budget and staff limitations allow, the public access television channel should be a presence at significant community events such as holiday parades, arts festivals, special town meetings, and major sporting events. Visibility at such events not only places public access in the context of community life but provides the subject matter for videotape footage that can be aired on the channel. And every venture into the community affords another opportunity to procure names and addresses to build up the public access television center's mailing list to use for future education and fund raising.

While it is generally advisable to maintain nonpartisanship and ideological neutrality, the world of politics provides public access television with other opportunities. It is almost universally acknowledged that commercial television stations do a poor job of covering local politics, generally, devoting the little time they have to superficial stories and soundbites.[3] Instead of waiting for producers to bring in programs with serious political content, public access television centers can proactively stage and broadcast all manner of forums, seminars, and debates. Public access proponents must encourage politicians and civic leaders to take advantage of the electronic soapbox that public access television provides (on an equal-time basis). Issue-oriented forums can be arranged in which average citizens can also have their say, either on tape, live in the studio, or by calling in.

Similarly, it is recommended that public access television centers should gravitate towards, rather than away from, community controversies. Again, it is important for an access operation to maintain its integrity as a neutral outlet and remain above the fray in terms of advocating for a particular position; to do otherwise might jeopardize public support. But this does not mean that the channel should not be used to bring expressions of divergent opinions on serious issues out of board rooms and municipal chambers and into the public eye. Opening up such debates to wider scrutiny and greater participation is a great public service that commercial broadcasters do not provide. Depending upon the topic, lively programs on meaningful issues should also attract viewers.

Another avenue for raising awareness about public access television is through marketing and public relations, and a first step in any marketing plan is to educate the organization's constituencies. Essential to the success of any public access television organization is the awareness of its staff, board of directors, users, viewers, and the community-at-large about the history and objectives of public access television. The history is important because it gives depth and meaning to the objectives of public access television. Unless the people involved in public access television know this history and how it has molded the objectives, it makes it very hard to value public access television. Often people get involved in public access television, either as a staff member, board member, user, or producer, without knowing much about why it exists. Educating these people about public access television will give them a stake in its future and motivate them to reach out to others.

In addition to educating staff and users about public access television, the general public also needs to be enlightened. Public access television advocates should do their best to have their service regarded as a public utility rather than as an entertainment option. Once the public discerns the importance of public access television centers to their communities as facilitators and purveyors of public discourse and civic involvement, the future of public access television will become more secure. As a few of the survey respondents noted, public access television can be a hard sell. And what makes a hard sell easier? Education regarding the need for the "product" being sold. How do people know they need public access television? How does anyone ever know they need something if they do not know that something exists? How do we know if we like public access television if we have never had public access television? You do not miss a service that you have never had. Doing outreach through speakers' bureaus, airing shows about the importance of public access, and lobbying government officials and media outlets can go a long way toward educating the community about the philosophic importance and practical advantages of public access television.

Compounding the awareness problem is that there is certainly no dearth of television watching. Trying to focus attention on public access television within the larger context of television is like trying to identify a single drop in a glass of water. Public access television proponents argue that there is a significant part of the television experience that most communities are missing, yet few people feel left out of the television process. If most Americans are consigned to a role of passive receiver of images and information, few seem to feel slighted or limited. And, of course, this is just the way that most corporate advertisers—the driving force behind most television programming—want it. The most desirable audience for advertising is captive, receptive, and (except for shopping) passive. This stands in direct contrast to the qualities that are valued in public access television.

One method of imparting information about public access television that has been shown to be effective is through a video documentary that succinctly traces the history of the local center or of the larger public access movement and illuminates the objectives of public access television. Such an informational video could be shown on public access channels, integrated into the public access television center's orientation meetings, and used by board members or other advocates as part of speaking engagements out in the community.[4]

FINANCIAL SECURITY AND FUND RAISING

Although the majority of funding most public access organizations receive is from the cable company or the local governmental entity, it is almost never enough. To achieve financial security, every public access center needs a fund raising plan. Various fund raising methods must be assessed, based on the center's current needs and resources. Several respondents remarked they had little time for fund raising. A fund raising plan, however, will make the fund raising process more efficient and will help staff, board members, and volunteers feel more comfortable with fund raising in general because they can see what has to be done and who is going to do it.

It is equally important to remember that 90 percent of private donations come from individuals and this is where most of the fund raising energies should be directed. This does not rule out grantwriting, but contributions and support by individuals are most important to the center's overall well-being, as well as to its bottom line.[5]

A necessary first step in developing the fund raising plan is the designation of a fund raising coordinator. This person can be a staff member, board member, or volunteer, but one individual should be responsible for overseeing this task. One of the primary responsibilities this person would accept is to facilitate the writing and implementation of the long-range fund raising plan. This does not mean that this person must do all of the work. Other staff, board members, and volunteers can be recruited for various tasks, but someone needs to be the coordinator. Otherwise, fund raising efforts are likely to suffer from disorganization and lack of focus.

The criteria for judging possible fund raising methods include the time required, the number of people needed, costs and potential returns, special knowledge that may be needed, obligations that may come with funds, the stability of the funding source, worst-case scenarios, and optimal results. The fund raising coordinator should assess each of these criteria honestly to determine if a particular task or method is right for the organization.[6]

After answering these questions, the fund raising coordinator should begin to outline the fund raising plan. It is essential to create a long-term plan, not just a strategy for the current year. Survey respondents reported various fund raising activities, but none mentioned having a fund raising plan per se. A fund raising plan should be the first step in any fund raising endeavor. The plan should delineate which strategies will be used and how they will be implemented. Some strategies that work for other, more traditional nonprofit organizations will not be appropriate for public access television centers.

Realistically, public access television centers should maximize earned income opportunities by charging or continuing to charge for memberships, classes, workshops, dubbing, and production services. Another source of earned income is the sale of merchandise such as blank videotapes, mugs, T-shirts, hats, bumper stickers, and pins. Only one-third of survey respondents reported employing earned income strategies as a method of fund raising. This is a relatively easy technique of raising funds that every public access television center could implement readily.

As mentioned earlier in this chapter, maintaining a mailing list is essential. The mailing list should include every member, board member, and staff member, as well as anyone and everyone who contacts the center. Opportunities for viewers to send in their names and addresses should be offered on a weekly or monthly basis by offering free items (mugs or bumper stickers for people who send in a postcard) or running contests on the channel. If possible, mailing lists should be obtained from groups with similar constituencies. Other small, local nonprofit organizations may be willing to share their membership lists. And finally, the mailing list must be maintained (updated and fine-tuned) weekly. Any mailing list becomes stale very quickly, and keeping it up to date requires constant attention as well as a good computer database. Most nonprofit organizations are only as good as their mailing lists and their ability to put them to use.

Part of every public access television center's fund raising plan should include an annual campaign with as many as twelve mailed requests every year. In addition, one special event can be planned each year if it can be expected to pay for itself, attract positive attention, and increase "psychic revenue." Of course, special events can demand a great deal of time, energy, and sometimes up-front money. Serious thought, soul-searching, and planning are necessary before undertaking such a project. If a special event is profitable and unique, it can be repeated every year.

A monthly newsletter can also help to raise funds and should be included in the plan. Some local access newsletters sell space for ads or messages. And every newsletter should include a request for donations as well as a form for people to fill out to offer suggestions or express their interest in public access television.

Joint projects with other nonprofits in the area should also be considered. If staff resources permit, other nonprofit organizations could pay the center to produce a videotape. Two nonprofit organizations could also write a joint grant proposal, to address a local need, denoting the kind of networking and interagency cooperation—synergy—that foundations and other funders value.

A fund raising plan can provide for a substantial role to be played by the board of directors. Every board member should not only be a member of the center but should make a dollar contribution as well—no one wants to give to an organization that is not supported, financially and every other way, by its own board members. It is beneficial for anyone representing the center to be able to state publicly that all board members have given money (of whatever amount) as well as time. The act of giving itself means commitment and serves to motivate the board members to participate in fund raising. In addition, every board member should participate in some way in the fund raising process. Board members can be enlisted to research and apply for grants, especially if they have some relevant expertise or experience.

Once a fund raising plan is written, it needs to be implemented. All staff and board members should be amenable to the plan, be invested in it, and be involved in its implementation. Without total support from staff, board members, users, and producers, a fund raising plan cannot be completely successful. But if everyone has been properly informed and educated, the center should have little problem gaining support.

As mentioned earlier, public access television centers can use their channels as a key component in the implementation of the fund raising plan. One of the suggestions from the survey was to record holiday or special occasion greetings for a small donation and air them at a special time—either once a day, once a week, or continuously—before the specific holiday. Other ways to use the channel to raise funds are to videotape biographies for people for a reasonable fee; televise an annual talent show and charge an entry fee for each entrant; hold a weekly dance party and charge admission; have a raffle on the channel; allow people to sponsor the channel for the day (they'll get an announcement on the air that they are the day sponsor); or hold a telethon. All of these projects can also serve to attract visitors to the access center and help build the mailing list.

MEDIA LITERACY PROGRAMS

People involved in public access television, whether staff, board members, producers, viewers, or funders, tend to be active, more critical viewers of all television programming. Awareness about how television works, technically, aesthetically, economically, and culturally, provides a raised level of consciousness about television.

Working with media literacy groups, schools and universities, and concerned citizens, public access television centers can become actively engaged in creating media literacy programs to air on their channels as well as to lend or sell to schools. (See Appendix 4 for media literacy organizations and resources.)

Improving media literacy involves educating people about the nature of television—about what makes up the television world.[7] Television is full of overt messages as well as covert or subliminal ones. Media literacy involves exposing both types of messages and laying bare the biases of television. These biases include bias through selection and omission; bias through placement; bias by headline; bias by photos, captions, and camera angles; bias through the use of names and titles; bias through statistics and crowd counts; bias by source control; and bias by word choice and tone. Exposing these biases allows for a clearer picture of television to emerge and for a deeper understanding of the importance of public access television.[8]

ALLIANCE FOR COMMUNITY MEDIA

As noted in Chapter 1, the Alliance for Community Media (originally named the National Federation of Local Cable Programmers) was founded in 1976 as a nonprofit, national membership organization. Currently it represents the interests of almost one thousand public, educational, and governmental access television organizations and public access Internet centers throughout the country. Membership in the Alliance can be important for securing the future of individual public access television organizations as well as the public access television movement. On the local public access television center level, a membership in the Alliance provides support services including technical assistance, regulatory updates, and opportunities to share information and expertise. Networking and education are facilitated primarily through national and regional conventions, through various special interest groups (such as trainers, volunteer producers, and government and educational access coordinators), and through its listserv. The Alliance also provides materials and information on community programming and national policy issues.[9]

On a national level, the Alliance is committed to "assuring everyone's access to electronic media." The Alliance accomplishes this by educating the public, building coalitions, supporting local organizing, monitoring the telecommunications industry, and advocating for the public's access to emerging media systems. In addition, the Alliance also promotes political, regulatory, and industry support for PEG access, primarily through its government relations program, public and press relations, the Alliance Public Policy Network and Council, fax broadcast services, Internet communication, and grassroots organizing. By becoming a member, a center can be a part of this organization and receive support via materials and consultation. Individuals also can receive support and, more importantly, be registered as one of a growing number of those who believe public access television is a valuable resource that every community should have.[10]

RELATIONSHIP WITH FUNDING SOURCES

Creating and maintaining a positive relationship with the center's primary funding sources is also critical. Local cable personnel, government officials, individual and corporate donors, and civic leaders need to be educated as to the benefits of public access television. Public access television is local, and it is the local programming dimension that distinguishes cable from the competition. Access centers can avail themselves of the opportunity to work in partnership with the cable company and the local government. For example, the center could videotape an event that the cable company is sponsoring and then put it on the channel, giving the cable company credit for their good citizenship. Local elected officials can be invited to appear on the channel, in political and nonpolitical contexts.

Another reason to maintain a good relationship with the cable company and local government officials is to lay the groundwork for future franchise negotiations and to get help for promotional purposes. The local government can also list public access television as a resource in public relations materials that it prints. The cable company's executive director and all the local elected officials should receive newsletters and other periodic updates on the center's activities. If a positive relationship exists with local government officials they are more likely to be more forceful advocates for public access during renegotiation of the franchise agreement with the cable company. Jim O'Brien, president of Jones Intercable Inc. of Englewood, Colorado, the nation's seventh-largest cable provider, stated in the *Wall Street Journal,* "If you're talking about a 500-channel universe, there may be great value in public-access channels in establishing local identity."[11] The ultimate goal is for these primary funding sources to see public access television as an asset to them personally, economically, and to the community at large.

LOBBY FOR INCREASED PUBLIC ACCESS
TELEVISION REGULATIONS

Public access television supporters can help insure the continued growth of public access television by working nationally, at the state level, and locally to have regulations implemented to protect present public access television regulations and to create new regulations to insure public access television on direct broadcast satellite (DBS) and other video delivery systems.

Because few local public access television operators, producers, and advocates have the time or proximity to lobby effectively at the federal level, membership in the Alliance can help citizens keep up with the regulatory environment and participate in organized lobbying efforts. At the state and local levels, knowledge of present and potential regulations will provide the background necessary to begin working and lobbying. In addition, developing relationships with elected officials at the state and local levels will also create an avenue for beginning discussions on the importance of public access television to the state and local communities.

As Bert Briller, former executive editor of the Television Information Office of the National Association of Broadcasters, put it, "The access channels must not be taken for granted, or abandoned. They need to be protected by specific inclusion in new media regulations, because they are vital to the development of a truly responsive and responsible television system."[12]

CONCLUSION

The twenty-first century is upon us. Although factors that are not yet clear (such as technological advances in fiber optics that could conceivably render the cable delivery system obsolete) may affect the future of public access television, there is good reason to believe that this media service—or something closely resembling it—will remain vital. In fact, the great strength of public access television— its fulfillment of the promise of democratic participation in the marketplace of ideas—is likely to become more valued, not less. Even though information can flow much faster, and in far greater quantities, via computer, telephone, or fax, none of these modes are local and geographically communal. Of all the media, public access television still holds the greatest potential for bringing communities together and binding them in shared knowledge and experience. Local control of and participation in television is also the best protection against the homogenization of the mass media. With the concentration of control of the global media in a shrinking number of corporate hands, public access television stands as one media institution that could and should remain free and fully democratic.

NOTES

1. Tony Schwartz, *The Responsive Chord*, (Garden City, NY: Anchor, 1973), 78.

2. Kim Klein, *Fund Raising for Social Change*, (Inverness, CA: Chardon Press, 1988), 9.

3. Doris A. Graber, *Mass Media and American Politics*, (Washington, DC: CQ Press, 1993), 348–49. See also Phyllis Kaniss, *The Media and the Mayor's Race*, (Bloomington, IN: Indiana University Press, 1995), 365, 370–73; and Phyllis Kaniss, *Making Local News*, (Chicago: University of Chicago Press, 1991), 6–7, 221, 231.

4. Most public access centers have an orientation meeting for people who are interested in becoming members. At these meetings, general information about public access and the specific policies and procedures of the center are discussed.

5. Ann Kaplan, ed., *Giving USA 1996, Annual Report on Philanthropy for the Year 1996*, (Norwalk, CT: AAFRC Trust for Philanthropy, 1997), 16–17.

6. Klein, 26; and Michael Seltzer, *Securing Your Organization's Future*, (New York: The Foundation Center, 1987), 399–456.

7. *Kids and TV: A Parents' Guide to TV Viewing*, Charlotte, NC: Public Affairs Division of Cablevision, n.d., 5.

8. Ibid., 9.

9. Alliance for Community Media at http://www.alliancecm.org/acmacm.htm

10. Ibid.

11. Anita Sharpe, "Television (A Special Report): What We Watch—Borrowed Time— Public Access Stations Have a Problem: Cable Companies Don't Want Them Anymore," *Wall Street Journal*, 9 September 1994, Eastern edition, sec. R, p. 12.

12. Bert Briller, "Accent on Access Television," *Television Quarterly* 28, no. 2 (Spring 1996): 58.

Appendix 1

Questionnaire and Data

SURVEY RESPONSES

QUESTION 1: Please describe your most successful fund raising activities.

1. Kiddie Telethon—eight hours of live community talent.

2. Funding received from public access fee—$173,000 and the balance is made up with franchise fee revenues. Walk-a-thon, benefit performance at local theatre, parking donation day from local county government, structured membership system.

3. No answer.

4. Sponsor fee, shows are sponsor only—$65 to $125 or more.

5. No answer. Franchise fees, support from library, sell sponsorships on programs and bulletin boards which brings in some funding.

6. No answer.

7. Boys/girls basketball tournament (high school).

8. Check-off campaign—a box on their bill where subscribers can check it off to give a dollar to the local public access station.

9. Ask local businesses for support on specific projects.

10. Suggested donations per tape for a copy of a community program such as high school graduation.

11. Sell videotapes of programs they have produced and activities that they recorded, such as football highlights, band and chorale concerts, prom, graduation, senior memory video (educational access).

12. Selling ads on bulletin boards and program channels.

13. Pass out flyers with cablecast times and order form, sell copies of games for $15 each. $4,000 in 1996—uses for volunteer development and for purchase of small items.

14. Capital campaign for new building (1.2 MK), major donor campaign (200K), on-air fund raiser (50K/year), on-air auctions (10K/year), concert series (15K/year).

15. No answer.

16. No answer.

17. No answer.

18. Softball tournament for kids to raise money for different youth organizations.

19. No answer.

20. Senior citizens ball with 16-piece orchestra—businesses donated door prizes.

21. No answer.

22. Miniature golf tournament raised $650.

23. No answer.

24. No answer.

25. Corporate underwriting and grants from fund raising for independent producers. Producers use PCTV as a conduit organization to help raise funds and PCTV takes 10 percent as a conduit fee. ($1,000–2,000/year) $24,000 grant from Telecommunications Education Fund to produce series of four live programs that disseminated important

consumer information to a target audience of disadvantaged African Americans. United Way Donor Option Program costs $75/year and generates $2,500/year. Awards events and tenth anniversary party. Both lost money.

26. Grants, annual large telethon in cooperation with another NPO for 26 hours—auction items and entertainment. Fun! Fun! Fun! eight hour telethon for PAC8 only—same format.

27. No answer.

28. No answer.

29. No answer.

30. No answer.

31. No answer.

32. No answer.

33. No answer.

34. No answer.

35. No answer.

36. No answer.

37. No answer.

38. High school sporting events with ad sponsorships—live coverage greatly receptive.

39. No answer.

40. No answer.

41. Direct requests via personal contacts with local business and organizations.

42. Becoming hired guns for clients who want promos or biographies.

43. No answer.

44. Direct appeal to cable viewers via bill stuffers, on-channel solicitations, underwriting from local businesses, organizations, and individuals, direct appeal to local church and other service organizations via letters.

45. No answer.

46. "Phonathon"—call every resident in town and ask them to allow us to add $1.00 to their cable bill each month. The cable company bills, collects and sends the money to us. We have about 3,000 residents and are receiving $1200 a month from this source.

47. Limited funding received for special projects.

48. Annual televised auction, selling tapes of PACT programming (high school graduation, parades, 1953 film about the town), volunteers hawk beer at local music festivals.

49. No answer.

50. No answer.

QUESTION 2: Please list any other income-generating activities.

1. All of the 5 percent franchise fee; producers fund payment of $5,000 to 6,000 per year.

2. Annual awards show ($4500), direct solicitation by board members to local business community.

3. Charge users for studio and editing time. Does not deter many people. They are breaking production records this year and the income makes up 20 to 25 percent of their budget ($10,000 to $12,000).

4. Money from county government for government shows ($930), monthly contribution from cable franchisee ($750), contribution by Calaveras Office of Education for our shows that depict school activities [no amount listed], and video workshops, membership fees.

5. Run copies of programs and rent equipment and editing facilities to non–public access users.

6. Sale of copies of programs.

7. Recreation[al] wrestling tournament.

8. No answer.

9. No answer.

10. Two percent gross revenues of annual income of our cable company as part of franchise agreement.

11. Christmas greeting videos shot in the studio with Christmas set, paid for by individuals ($1 each/$5 minimum). All put on one tape and played continuously 24 hours a day for the week before Christmas. The whole city watches them over and over. All shot in one week. Brought in $250 the first year, $500 the second year, $700 the third year. This utilizes what we do (TV) and gets people involved and is very positive.

12. No answer.

13. Get sponsors to donate food to volunteers for money making shoots.

14. Membership—Internet access, conducting ISDN leasing, class fees, production services, book and record sale, equipment auction.

15. No answer.

16. No answer.

17. No answer.

18. Make copies of programs for public.

19. No answer.

20. No answer.

21. No answer.

22. Charge tape use fees and workshop fees.

23. Social service agencies have donated equipment through the nonprofit advisory council.

24. Leased access playback.

25. $.25 per city cable subscriber, $20 enrollment fee, $52/year to producers to use facility ($11,000/year), charge for workshops ($5 to $15 each; $2,000/year), charge for videotape and dubbing ($6,000/year).

26. Underwriting community calendar sections, sponsorship of shows and series, outside production, camera rental, membership fees, and children's video classes every Wednesday afternoon.

27. No answer.

28. No answer.

29. No answer.

30. No answer.

31. No answer.

32. No answer.

33. No answer.

34. No answer.

35. No answer.

36. No answer.

37. No answer.

38. Industrial videos and dubs.

39. Producers solicit advertising underwriters. Public access center is not involved.

40. Underwriting of programming, duplication of programs.

41. Production-related donations and sponsorships, tape copy sales, general public donations.

42. Hired guns, dubbing/videotape copying services, consultants, bartering for bulletin board air time with a radio station, Internet provider and parties and bar mitzvahs.

43. Low-cost programming from PBS as well as other distributors, receive free PSAs on a regular basis.

44. Sale of copies of tapes.

45. Corporate underwriting for general station purposes. Local business underwriting specific to live sports broadcasts.

46. Tag sales, celebrity reception, tennis tournaments, etc. All have been a lot of work and some fun, but none have been as lucrative as the phone calls.

47. Earned income: classes, memberships, interest.

48. Project-oriented grant writing ($18,000 over 3 years). Local foundation grant writing. Charge fees to local governments for production costs associated with recording and telecasting their meetings ($15,000).

49. Sell new S-VHS tapes—charge for memberships and classes.

50. In-kind contributions—backdrops, flower arrangements, tapes.

QUESTION 3: What is your approximate annual budget?

1. $90,000
2. $212,000
3. $50,000

4. $28,000
5. $110,000
6. $210,000

7. $10,000

8. $20,000

9. $475,000

10. $50,000

11. $0

12. $85,000

13. No answer.

14. $1,200,0000

15. $470,000

16. $2,000,0000

17. $40,000

18. $64,000

19. $20,000

20. $72,000

21. No answer.

22. $65,000

23. $170,000

24. $200,000

25. $360,000

26. $60,000

27. No answer.

28. $10,000

29. $30,000

30. $8,000

31. No answer.

32. No answer.

33. No answer.

34. $124,000

35. $90,000

36. No answer

37. No answer.

38. $80,000

39. No answer.

40. $85,000

41. $8,000

42. $164,400

43. $6,000

44. $100,000

45. $130,000

46. $41,000

47. $1,600,000

48. $143,000

49. $225,000

50. No answer.

QUESTION 4: From what sources is your center funded and what percentage of your annual budget comes from each source?

1. 5% franchise fee (90,000)

2. Public access fee $173,000—franchise fee $39,000 ($212,000)

3. Municipal franchise fees 40%; grants 20%; membership/fund raising 15%; production fees 22%; misc. 3% ($50,000)

4. County Office of Education 85%; cable company 10%; county government 5%

5. Franchise fee 40%; cable company grant 20%; sponsorships 5%; copying tapes and equipment rental 5%; library operating budget 30%

6. Funded by franchise agreement revenues

7. Municipal government 100%

8. 100% funded by cable company

9. Franchise fees 55%; community service fee 44%; contractual income 5%; interest 4%, reimbursements 1%

10. 2% of gross revenue of cable company
11. City schools general fund 50%; activity fund 50%
12. 5% fee from cable company 90%; ads 10%
13. 100% from city
14. Franchise fees are 33% of budget; fund raising and earned income is 67%
15. $20,000 from membership and workshop fees; 1.5% of gross revenue of cable company
16. 90% cable company; 10% interest
17. 100% fielded by the college
18. 100% franchise agreement
19. Township government appropriation
20. 100% from cable company
21. 100% from cable company
22. 100% cable company
23. 100% cable company
24. 80% funded by the city from the franchise fee; 20% funded by cable company.
25. 80% funded by cable company.
26. 54% franchise through county ($32,000); 17% grant ($10,000); 29% other
27. 100% cable company
28. 100% funded by franchise agreement revenues
29. 100% from cable company operating budget
30. No answer.
31. No answer.
32. No answer.
33. No answer.
34. 100% from franchise fees.
35. 70% community college; 30% cable company
36. No answer.
37. No answer.
38. 100% from cable company
39. No answer.
40. 99% from cable from the franchise; 5% cable fees returned to municipality
41. 95% city; 5% donations
42. 55% of 5% franchise fee = 96% of budget
43. 100% from university
44. 70% county tax dollars; 11% grant; 8% cable TV company; 11% contributions and underwriting
45. 96% contract with Cablevision; and 4% underwriting

46. 55% cable company; 4% town government; 32% subscriber contributions; 9% other
47. 5% from cable; 75% grants-underwriting-contributions; 10% interest
48. 60% city; 20% cable company and ten other governmental bodies; 10% earned income
49. 78% direct grant from cable company (not franchise fee); 22% grant from city
50. 30% of the 5% franchise fee from the cable company

QUESTION 5: In what ways have funding sources impacted your programming? Are there any noticeable changes in programming in the last few years and have any of these resulted in a change of fund raising?

1. As viewer penetration increases our revenues increase, our city has been growing and this has a positive effect on our budget.
2. No answer.
3. Municipalities have doubled the amount of franchise fees they contribute, so government programming has increased. Professionals are spending money on production for self-interest. We are experimenting with production fees to get community groups involved.
4. Continuously increasing the number of TV shows that generate income. Submit programs to cable company which plays them on a 24-hour/week schedule, programs deal with people and events in the county.
5. The more money, the better the programming. Through additional franchise fees we were able to move into a larger space and purchase more equipment, allowing more producers to work on programs.
6. Budget has been used to purchase equipment that's improved technical quality of our programs.
7. Limited to municipal funds, no advertising or fund raising allowed anymore. No change in programming.
8. Only impact on programming is lack of personnel.
9. Funding increased last year with a new franchise, so service has increased.
10. No answer.
11. Lack of finds have resulted in many limitations on our programming capabilities, not the least of which is our woefully ancient equipment. We shoot and edit on Betamax 1, occasionally on standard 3/4″ U-matic. Repairs of broken equipment [are] very difficult because of its obsolescence. The need for my services in other curricula takes me away from television production, thereby limiting the number of programs produced. However, we average 36 original programs each school year. Approximately one per week. There have been no noticeable changes in programming, but an improvement when we were able to purchase a Video Toaster.
12. No answer.

13. No answer.

14. Clear distinction between programming and fund raising.

15. No answer.

16. No answer.

17. We support distance learning activities. Funding has increased as distance learning has become a more and more important part of our mission.

18. No answer.

19. Political interference occasionally.

20. Would like to have a larger budget, which would enable us to do more.

21. No answer.

22. No answer.

23. There was a demand for news. Now produce nightly newscast.

24. All in-house programming produced commercial free. In the last few years city wants to fund less so they can have more money without raising taxes.

25. Funding has allowed us to make great improvements in quality of equipment and set pieces used to produce programming. The noticeable changes are increased programming, more efficient use of facilities, better quality video and editing; better audio; improved station signal, live programming capability; the ability to receive satellite transmissions and increased numbers of programs.

26. Adult and children's workshops have resulted in more programming—so has convincing corporations to sponsor events.

27. No answer.

28. No answer.

29. No answer.

30. No answer.

31. No answer.

32. No answer.

33. No answer.

34. No answer.

35. No answer.

36. No answer.

37. No answer.

38. No answer.

39. No answer.

40. Less people moving into municipality less franchise fees. Underwriting and other service fees help to maintain and increase programming.

41. No changes, but being on the purse strings of the government means we need to take into account their wishes over general public requests.

42. If you have minimal funding, you cannot purchase the electronic equipment you need. Usually it becomes piecemeal, a little of this, this year, a little of that, the next

year. So quality, or a similar look [to that] the local stations have, does not happen. The equipment needs to be maintained. Staffing ends up to be critical, the staff person is made to do more with less and salaries compete with overhead and equipment dollars. Volunteers have less to use so scheduling and creating slows to a crawl and less shows are produced. The past four to five years we have noticed a drop in willingness to barter or donate. Reagan's trickledown theory has not worked. The change in programming fluctuates. Some local businesses do not like something that have a tendency to want to kill the messenger.

43. Our cable station is not broadcasting educational programming as we would like to do because we lack essential funds for equipment, maintenance, installation, and personnel to operate the cable station.

44. Had to do fundraising to add additional staff and to purchase any new equipment. Both of these have had a large impact on increasing the amount of programming.

45. No answer.

46. Funding sources have no impact on programming. We don't see any significant changes in programming, but the *quality* of the programs has improved due to better equipment and more experience in the technical production skills.

47. No in terms of fund raising. Funding sources limit programming to amount of support. More dollars equals more programming and services

48. We have seen a rapid growth in membership and programming in recent years, without growth in staff. We do almost no proactive planning in programming. Consequently we have a lack of good programming for some interests and abundance in others, e.g., out of sixty hours, eight is from religious institutions, but we have about an hour of programming for seniors and about an hour total for all ethnic programming. There have been significant changes in programming in the last few years. No "programming adventures." We do have one ultraconservative producer who managed to ire a banker on the city council, but that is just a small part of our problems with the city council.

49. No answer.

50. Having no operating budget has meant little or no training for community residents, no outreach, no offsite activity unless someone has their own camera, limited programming. However, even under these conditions we have managed to broadcast two nights a week for two hours, repeated the following days at noon, for nearly five years. We actually started out with three hours a week. People have begun to know there is such a thing as access but we can't offer them much being just a few people with no studio and no money.

QUESTION 6: What problems if any have you faced with fund raising and funding?

1. We do little fund raising.

2. No answer.

3. Obviously, recessions are never good for nonprofits. We barely survived the early 1990s. The station is in an area (suburbs of NYC) that is saturated with nonprofits

and competition for dollars is keen, strong base of support in the community which always comes through when we ask for help.

4. Money is tight, especially in a small rural county like ours. We consider it a problem that only people who have money to sponsor or who find paying sponsors can expect to get productions made.

5. Not too many up to this point. We could always use more money, of course.

6. We are limited to the franchise fees and do not get support from the city's general fund. Also, we have not yet had fund raisers or telethons.

7. Convincing borough council to increase funding due to rising costs.

8. No answer.

9. No answer.

10. Due to limited number of businesses in our small community, we receive very little in donations from community-at-large.

11. The only major problem is time. I am the only adult in the program, so fund raising adds additional responsibilities to an already crowded schedule.

12. No time to devote to fund raising or programming for that purpose.

13. No answer.

14. Public access isn't a "soft" touch for fund raising. Some feel franchise fees should be enough.

15. No answer.

16. No answer.

17. No answer.

18. No answer.

19. Continually must convince township of the value of public access.

20. We are not primarily in fund raising. We serve our community organizations and help them with fundraising.

21. No answer.

22. Lack of interest by the fundraisers and overall low involvement in the program. However, even when the program was active in the past, there was very little fund raising.

23. None. The public does not mind an increase because the understand the value.

24. Not allowed raising funds.

25. Like most nonprofit organizations, raising money is getting harder and harder as foundations and corporations tightens their purse strings. We have experienced an attitude from foundations and corporations that public access television is a luxury and since we're not feeding the hungry or taking care of the homeless, money doesn't flow freely. Now the biggest problem is getting money to fund the purchase of equipment and integrating Internet into our services.

26. Not enough time, too busy managing to go after funding. Had to send assistant to grantwriting school and hire a marketing person.

27. No answer.

28. No answer.

29. No answer.

30. No answer.

31. No answer.

32. No answer.

33. No answer.

34. No answer.

35. No answer.

36. No answer.

37. No answer.

38. Limited staff members working local origination. More staff time was devoted to ad-insertion production for other cable channels.

39. No answer.

40. Finding grant money is difficult.

41. We don't have funding to pay a fundraising staff, which makes it hard to do much active fundraising. Volunteer time spent fund raising helps, but most volunteers want to produce shows rather than "work."

42. Raising dollars is an art form. We are still in the infancy stage. We have a problem fitting into the square pegs criteria for funding. We fall through the cracks. We are public, governmental and educational access bona fide SOlc.3 nonprofit. We have letters of rejection, no answer, or do not qualify. Fund raising is a long slow arduous journey we have no expertise in.

43. Lack funds needed funds for equipment, maintenance, and installation. Also lack funds for programming and needed personnel to operate the cable system.

44. We are funded primarily by county government. Because we are a nonessential service and some do not appreciate our service, our funds have always been capped. We have had to seek additional funding since our inception.

45. Establishing a clear public image of what we are what we do, and what we are NOT.

46. The "bake sale" approach to fund raising is simply not very productive—very small returns for a lot of work. Equipment is very expensive and has a limited life expectancy when used by volunteer amateurs.

47. We are [a] fiscally sound organization with guaranteed payments from cable franchise. Funders look for "poorer" organizations to fund. We are also a technical assistance provider and media. Two more strikes against us in the funding arena.

48. Three years ago, the City Library that had served as our host since 1978, told us that they no longer had room for PACT. We were able to find a donor who would give us space in a city ten miles away that was in the Eau Claire cable (fiber) system. ED City Council opted to move us to an industrial mall in E.C. and pay our rent. We negotiated a five-year lease on our new facility, built to our specs in November 1995.

49. Need more funding. Can't get organized.

50. No answer.

QUESTION 7: What types of programming do you cablecast and what percentage of your total programming does each type comprise?

1. Public, educational, governmental, children's.

2. No answer.

3. Government programming 30%; news 5%; talk shows 40%; on-location and other programming 5%; church programming 30%

4. Hobbies/community: parades, remarkable people, sports, business, development, fairs, school teachers, students, school restaurant, classroom activities, football, basketball, superintendent messages, monthly show with supervisors, presentations about government departments.

5. Talk 30%; religious 25%; town meetings 15%; town events 15%; sports 5%; entertainment and misc. 10%

6. Government 10%; religious 25%; sports 15%; entertainment 20%; talk 30%

7. Sports 50%; public information 25%; local government 25%

8. Our programming has complete variety. We are public, educational, and governmental. I am required by law to program just about anything.

9. Public access 78%; educational access 12%; and governmental 10%

10. 100% community accesses programming.

11. Sports 65%; academics 10%; concerts 10%; community (Supt.'s report, forums, debates) 8%; Feature stories 7%

12. Public affairs 20%; sports 50%; special events 20%; talk 5%; misc. 5%

13. No answer.

14. Religious 30%; public affairs 20%; sports 10%; entertainment 30%; misc. 10%

15. We cablecast all types, depending on the interest of the three hundred members. At each given time about one third of membership produce programs. Religious 15%; political viewpoint 20%; Senior issues 2%; gay 2%; other languages 4%; health 10%; entertainment 30%; misc. (cooking, travel, special interests) 17%

16. Informative 22%; entertainment 21%; art 12%; religious 8%; minority 13%; public affiairs 4%; children 3%; misc. 17%; mature 1%

17. Credit telecourses 60–70%; Student orientation/information 10–20%; community programming 10–20%; misc. 10–20%

18. Religious 10%; sports 10%; informational 50%; musical 20%; misc. 10% School Channel—Musicals 20%; sports 20%; information 40%; plays/skits 20%

19. General informational and school-related programs and events.

20. Local organization programming 95%; commercial prograrnming 5%

21. Religious 75%; magazine specialty 25%

22. Information and issue 15%; entertainment 0%; religious 50%; spanish 12%

23. News 4%; education 6%; gov't 3%; public affairs 16%; inspirational 2%; kids 13%; sports 5%; religion 9%; entertainment 12%; satellite 30%

24. Religious 85%; leased access 5%; govemmental 10%

25. No answer.

26. Public/community 70%; educational 20%; government 10%

27. Religious 48%; sports talk 19%; political talk 16%; public affairs 16%; misc. 1%.

28. Crafts 10%; Talk 20%; Government 10%; religious 50%; informative 10%; Arts 8%; business 1%; craft 1%; public affairs 23%; education 18%; political 3%; govemment 18%; health 1%; individual interest 13%; ethnic 2%; religious 1%; public service 8%; fillers 1%; and sports 1%

29. Talk/information 50%; sports 25%; entertainment/misc. 25%

30. School activities, educational/informational programs

31. No answer.

32. No answer.

33. No answer.

34. No answer.

35. Telecourses 60%; local college news 10%; music events 15%

36. No answer.

37. No answer.

38. City meetings 10%; sporting events 10%; in-studio productions 20%; community events 30%; Access program bicycle tapes 20%; cable promotions 10%

39. Educational, public access and government access—public access 20%; educational and governmental 80%

40. Community events 44%; local 29%; religious 17%; imported 10%

41. Public meetings 30%; events 25%; informational/inspirational 25%; entertainment 20%

42. Religious 38%; entertainment 20%; political 14%; educational 7%; sports 6%; cultural 6%; promotional 5%; PSAs 3%; misc. 1%

43. No answer.

44. Wide variety of governmental and public access

45. 3 channels: b3 is 100% governmental, i.e., civic meetings, city council, etc.; 5b [is] educational, i.e. daytime from state satellite network, other materials from colleges and schools, some courses for adult education; 3b is general public channel, i.e. religious, current affairs, sports, hobbies, music, broad variety.

46. Locally produced interviews on special interest shows 48%; town meetings 23%; local high school sports 11%; outside tapes 15%; religious 3%

47. No answer.

48. No answer.

49. Religious 42%; entertainment 25%; art/culture/music 10%; other 15%; public affairs 5%; mature 3%

50. Comedy 14%; documentary 8%; entertainment 8%; informative 40%; music 11%; performance 2%; sports 12%; talk 7%.

QUESTION 8: How many subscribers does your cable system currently have?

1. 4,500	26. 4,050
2. 32,000	27. 10,000
3. 24,000	28. 10,503
4. 8,500	29. 26,000
5. 13,500	30. No answer.
6. 14,000	31. No answer.
7. 3,200	32. 1,500
8. 62,000	33. No answer.
9. 13,450	34. 11,000
10. 6,000	35. No answer.
11. No answer.	36. No answer.
12. 5,000	37. No answer.
13. No answer.	38. 20,000
14. 120,000	39. 40,000
15. 66,000	40. 6,000
16. 500,000	41. 18,000
17. 70,000	42. 24,000
18. 12,000	43. 11,000
19. No answer.	44. 6,600
20. 38,500	45. 10,500
21. 30,000	46. 6,000
22. 20,000	47. 355,000
23. 28,500	48. 26,000
24. 78,000	49. 54,000
25. 105,000	50. 20,000

QUESTION 9: How many active producers does your center have?

1. 30	8. 120
2. 30	9. 30
3. 25	10. 25
4. 3	11. 1
5. 100	12. 3
6. 170	13. No answer.
7. 4	14. 75

15. 90–100
16. 2,000
17. 2
18. 30
19. 5+
20. 2
21. 24
22. 50
23. 34–79
24. 30
25. 300
26. 54
27. 17
28. 18
29. 1
30. No answer.
31. No answer.
32. No answer.
33. No answer.
34. No answer.
35. No answer.
36. No answer.
37. 8–10
38. No answer.
39. 20
40. 30
41. 12–25
42. 2
43. 50–100
44. No answer.
45. 8
46. 700 (certified users)
47. 110
48. 30
49. 7
50. 20,000

QUESTION 10: How many hours do you cablecast each week? How many hours are produced locally?

1. 130; 95%
2. No answer.
3. 30–35; 5–6 new programming
4. 24 hours local programming
5. 100; 20–30
6. 126; 65%
7. 5; 5
8. 70; 40
9. 166; 166
10. 168; 1–5
11. 4; 3.5
12. 20–25; 15–20
13. No answer.
14. 140; 40
15. 70; 65
16. 56; 90%
17. 74; 2/3
18. 88; 87
19. 9; 9
20. 56; 10
21. 15; 3
22. 44; 1/5
23. 65–85, and 65–85
24. 56; 45
25. 92; 92
26. 168; 80%
27. 16; 13.5
28. 24; 10
29. 20–25; 15+
30. 52; 100%
31. No answer.
32. No answer.
33. No answer.
34. No answer.

35. 75; 72

36. No answer.

37. No answer.

38. 40; 75%

39. 84; 5

40. 100; 98

41. No answer.

42. 135; 67%

43. 0; 0

44. 70+; 60+

45. 45–55 on public 85–90%; 45–50 on education 20%

46. 42 programming [hours], community calendar runs the rest of the time; 36

47. 5 channels at 165 hours/week; 70–80%

48. 67; 45

49. 60; 50+

50. 8; 99%

QUESTION 11: How do you generate viewers and producers?

1. By involving children and the community. People like to see themselves and their friends on television.

2. Citiguide, homepage, recreation reporter, word-of-mouth, annual awards program, participation in regional and national organizations, cross-channel promotion.

3. Viewers are generated through press releases in the local papers. We find that if they watch one show, they usually stick around for the next show. Many of our producers have approached us—we find that we rarely need to recruit producers. Word-of-mouth is also very strong in the community.

4. Good quality of shows of local interest do create an optimal amount of viewers. Producers are more difficult to find.

5. Word-of-mouth, channel surfing. Most everybody in this area knows who we are. We do programs about public access and we have a newsletter. We put notices in the newspaper and occasional radio programs.

6. Through promotion in other media and on our station.

7. Access calendar, word-of-mouth.

8. Commercial, press release, training workshops, open house.

9. Heavy PR in local newspapers, promos on our channel.

10. Press releases and articles in local papers.

11. Producers we do not generate, except for those who take the class. Programs are occasionally publicized in the local newspaper and on the local radio station, consistently over the school PA announcements, and on our 24-hour-a-day bulletin board on our dedicated channel.

12. Give the community what it wants. Don't try to establish your own format.

13. No answer.

14. Cross promotion on community radio, Internet, local ads avails on cable system ads.

15. List programs in newspaper, local TV guide, on-air preview channel, computer-generated program loop. We do our outreach through local colleges, high schools, etc.—service groups, but most come word-of-mouth from existing members.

16. Newsletter, messages on cable channels, community presentations, training workshops, community based training workshops, website.

17. No answer.

18. Educating the public about public access, do[ing] internships with university, hav[ing] high school students come in and get credit on how to use equipment, by doing good programs about community, providing a variety of programs, by taping out in the community. Had over seven hundred new programs last year.

19. We provide production facility for local public access.

20. Ads in paper and on community bulletin board.

21. Community billboard announcements and on-air disclaimers.

22. Announcements on the channel, news releases, public events, public speaking. There is a deep-rooted belief in the importance of public access to the media which cannot be determined solely by looking at the output of the programmers. The use of the channels may necessarily be by a very few. If so, then that's the way it should be. The existence of public access TV is more important than what it does, perhaps because of what it might do, but probably because we have [the] right to it. It should be there when we want it.

23. Cross-channel spots, news releases, local faces and places always on TV.

24. Since we're noncommercial, ratings are not important, most idle time is spent promoting other revenue-producing channels.

25. Word-of-mouth, on-air promos, newspaper ads and a monthly ad in the cable guide.

26. Lots of advertising and promotions—also workshops—every year we do a telethon we get more viewers and production that stick with us.

27. Word-of-mouth mostly. Some in-house promotion of shows via community bulletin board channels. Producers come to us.

28. Advertise workshops, word-of-mouth, producers put out own press releases about their shows. Viewers are generated by reading these press releases and our access channel is on basic service. We won't actively seek new programming.

29. Cross-channel promotion.

30. Advertise through schools.

31. No answer.

32. No answer.

33. No answer.

34. No answer.

35. No answer.

36. No answer.

37. No answer.

38. We generate viewers from TV8 schedule listings, Prevue Guide channel and newspaper listing. There has not been any priority on generating producers over the last couple of years.

39. Our schedule in local paper as part of weekly listings, we send out program flyer to about one thousand viewers each month. Producers are encouraged by word-of-mouth. There is no direct solicitation of programs or producers.

40. Advertise schedule in newspaper, posted in community, library, etc. Located in a high school, advertise on station, invite community service groups in to station.

41. No answer.

42. We generate viewers by having schedules, live call ins, each show produces its own following in the scheduling of programs, word-of-mouth works real well, placement of our signal at local conventions, art groups, nonprofits, talks to fraternal groups and businesses. We beat the bushes for producers, mostly middle and high schoolers, college students, nonprofits.

43. Employs two producers to produce videos that pertain to or promote the university and channel. They will also produce and direct local programming.

44. By word-of-mouth. By using other local media for announcements and listings (free services only). By posting schedules.

45. For producers we have a PR program including brochures, a six-minute video to garner recruits.

46. We generate viewers by putting on programs of local interest. We generate producers by running workshops and by word-of-mouth.

47. Respond to community need, optimize use of channels, implement services that are viewer- and user-friendly, establish accessible services with a low threshold for entry.

48. Mostly it just kind of happens. We try to do a viewership survey every three years although we're a year behind right now. (Let me know if you would like a copy.)

49. Article in newspapers. Word-of-mouth. Program listing in newspaper's People and Places section.

50. The newspaper publishes our schedule. The government access channel is basically a bulletin board and we put the schedule on that. Word of mouth. Through guests. Producers: Anyone who shows up and wants to get involved is welcomed "with open arms." However, without a budget and a coordinator we can't train people. The cable company last ran a class in April of 1994, though we tried to get them to do more and there were people who contact[ed] them seeking a class. A few people got fed up and just came when we were taping and learned on the job.

QUESTION 12: Is there anything I have not already raised that you would like to share with me?

1. As long as the cable industry remains strong and our franchise fees are sufficient to support cable access in Sun Prairie, the need to look for additional funds will not be necessary. If the revenues decrease due to satellite dishes, video dial tone or other technologies, we will have to look for additional source of revenues. We are exploring the possibility of writing for grants and qualifying for participation in the Universal Service Funding program as well as increasing local fund raising activities.

2. We are exploring changing the focus [from] 80 to 90% for the independent producer and 10 to 20% for the nonprofit organization to 80 to 90% for the nonprofit and 10 to 20% for the independent producer. The change is due to the low usage, low viewers, and the need to do more for the nonprofit community in promoting their services.

3. I think that as cable revenues have declined over the last few years (and therefore franchise fees), public access centers have seen a small decline over the last few

years. It is imperative for access centers to begin to increase the number of sources for revenue. We have had success in working with other nonprofits on joint grants. These are mutually beneficial prospects that provide much publicity for both organizations. Granters like to fund these projects.

4. No answer.

5. We have not relied on fund raising. Hopefully, it will not come that—it would take up much of our time, instead of working with producers. We try to make ourselves invaluable to the community in order to insure fixture finding through grants and fees.

6. We are a public/governmental access TV station, operated by the city of Midland-MCTV 3 & 5.

7. No answer.

8. TCI has seven towns in its franchise. Each town has its own facility funded by TCI. Each town has three channels designated for public access. 18, public; 19, educational; 20, government; 21, regional and services all seven towns. Each town's 18, 19, 20 will only generate information pertaining to that town.

9. No answer.

10. No answer.

11. No answer.

12. All local studios should be located in high school. That's where your help is.

13. No answer.

14. Community radio hired a fund Dev. Dir. as second position on state. PEG access doesn't hire fund raisers. Franchise fees should be used as a match for fund raising.

15. Visit our website at www.comtv.com, email at www.comtv@comtv.com.

16. No answer.

17. No answer.

18. No answer.

19. No answer.

20. No answer.

21. No answer.

22. No answer.

23. No answer.

24. With the exception of extremists such as hate groups or naked talk shows from California and New York, most all public access shows are decent and sincere and they are the only places on earth where the average person can access mass media without censorship.

25. No answer.

26. When you start growing by leaps and bounds as we have the last four years, you run out of resources: Be careful what you pray for!

27. No one is denied access unless they are not local franchise area residents.

28. No answer.

29. We aren't a public access facility. Hence, the public can't come in and use the equipment, etc. Because of this, a lot of your questions were not applicable.

30. No answer.

31. No answer.

32. No answer.

33. No answer.

34. No answer.

35. No answer.

36. No answer.

37. No answer.

38. A recent newspaper article stated that DBS will be getting involved with local programming to challenge cable companies. Do you have information that might lend to support this?

39. No answer.

40. No answer.

41. No answer.

42. We figure our initial growth and our continued development is tied to this god called money. Our growth was slowed considerably and some staff were overburdened with trying to meet the public's need for offering reasonable services. If one machine breaks down or needs repair we experience delays and in some cases monetary shortfalls. However, all is not despair, we do manage to function well and increase the volunteer and viewer base. (fundage sucks!)

43. I feel that you failed to take into account that some educational access cable stations have to depend on free or low-cost types of programming/PSAs.

44. Ours is a unique situation, as we are in a rural area serving seventeen little towns spread out over seventy miles distance. Our cable company is cooperatively owned, our situation is quite atypical. The cable company likes us, but has no real profits to share with us and no franchise agreements in the typical sense.

45. We are served by not one commercial or public TV station in this area west of Boston so we are the only TV in town with local reflection. This has determined our role to be dual—traditional access AND local community broadcast station.

46. No answer.

47. No answer.

48. No answer.

49. No answer.

50. We are a small group of volunteers who named ourselves C.A.C.T.US a year or so ago so we could get a better identity. It's Concord Area Community TV is US. Grammar is correct, but CACTWE just sounded too strange. WE think access can be of great benefit to a community. We come together with different philosophies and visions and have supported each other because we see real value in access plus it gives us an opportunity for doing something we also enjoy. It's been a long struggle and it isn't over yet but it's worth the effort.

Appendix 2

Federal Laws Regarding Public Access Procedures and Content

The following is the current federal law concerning public, educational, and governmental access content, facilities, and procedures. Please see state law, local ordinances, or the operating franchise agreement for any further procedures or restrictions.

1934 COMMUNICATIONS ACT

(as amended by 1984, 1992 and 1996 Acts)

SEC. 522. Definitions—For purposes of this subchapter

(1) the term "activated channels" means those channels engineered at the headend of a cable system for the provision of services generally available to residential subscribers of the cable system, regardless of whether such services actually are provided, including any channel designated for *public*, educational, or governmental use;

(2) the term "affiliate," when used in relation to any person, means another person who owns or controls, is owned or controlled by, or is under common ownership or control with, such person;

(3) the term "basic cable service" means any service tier which includes the retransmission of local television broadcast signals;

(4) the term "cable channel" or "channel" means a portion of the electromagnetic frequency spectrum which is used in a cable system and which is capable of delivering a television channel (as television channel is defined by the Commission by regulation);

(5) the term "cable operator" means any person or group of persons:

(A) who provides cable service over a cable system and directly or through one or more affiliates owns a significant interest in such cable system, or

(B) who otherwise controls or is responsible for, through any arrangement, the management and operation of such a cable system;

(6) the term "cable service" means—

(A) the one-way transmission to subscribers of

(i) video programming, or

(ii) other programming service, and

(B) subscriber interaction, if any, which is required for the selection or use of such video programming or other programming service;

(7) the term "cable system" means a facility, consisting of a set of closed transmission paths and associated signal generation, reception, and control equipment that is designed to provide cable service which includes video programming and which is provided to multiple subscribers within a community, but such term does not include:

(A) a facility that serves only to retransmit the television signals of one or more television broadcast stations;

(B) a facility that serves subscribers without using any public right-of-way;

(C) a facility of a common carrier which is subject, in whole or in part, to the provisions of subchapter II of this chapter, except that such facility shall be considered a cable system (other than for purposes of section 541(c) of this title) to the extent such facility is used in the transmission of video programming directly to subscribers, unless the extent of such use is solely to provide interactive on-demand services;

(D) an open video system that complies with section 573 of this title; or

(E) any facilities of any electric utility used solely for operating its electric utility system;

(8) the term "Federal agency" means any agency of the United States, including the Commission;

(9) the term "franchise" means an initial authorization, or renewal thereof (including a renewal of an authorization which has been granted subject to section 546 of this title), issued by a franchising authority, whether such authorization is designated as a franchise, permit, license, resolution, contract, certificate, agreement, or otherwise, which authorizes the construction or operation of a cable system;

(10) the term "franchising authority" means any governmental entity empowered by Federal, State, or local law to grant a franchise;

(11) the term "grade B contour" means the field strength of a television broadcast station computed in accordance with regulations promulgated by the Commission;

(12) the term "interactive on-demand services" means a service providing video programming to subscribers over switched networks on an on-demand, point-to-point basis, but does not include services providing video programming prescheduled by the programming provider;

(13) the term "multichannel video programming distributor" means a person such as, but not limited to, a cable operator, a multichannel multipoint distribution service, a direct broadcast satellite service, or a television receive-only satellite program distributor, who makes available for purchase, by subscribers or customers, multiple channels of video programming;

(14) the term "other programming service" means information that a cable operator makes available to all subscribers generally;

(15) the term "person" means an individual, partnership, association, joint stock company, trust, corporation, or governmental entity;

(16) the term "*public*, educational, or governmental access facilities" means— (A) channel capacity designated for *public*, educational, orgovernmental use; and (B) facilities and equipment for the use of such channel capacity;

(17) the term "service tier" means a category of cable service or other services provided by a cable operator and for which a separate rate is charged by the cable operator;

(18) the term "State" means any State, or political subdivision, or agency thereof;

(19) the term "usable activated channels" means activated channels of a cable system, except those channels whose use for the distribution of broadcast signals would conflict with technical and safety regulations as determined by the Commission; and

(20) the term "video programming" means programming provided by, or generally considered comparable to programming provided by, a television broadcast station.

SEC. 531. Cable channels for *public*, educational, or governmental use

(a) A franchising authority may establish requirements in a franchise with respect to the designation or use of channel capacity for *public*, educational, or governmental use only to the extent provided in this section.

(b) A franchising authority may in its request for proposals require as part of a franchise, and may require as part of a cable operator's proposal for a franchise renewal, subject to section 626, that channel capacity be designated for *public*, educational, or governmental use, and channel capacity on institutional networks be designated for educational or governmental use, and may require rules and procedures for the use of the channel capacity designated pursuant to this section.

(c) A franchising authority may enforce any requirement in any franchise regarding the providing or use of such channel capacity. Such enforcement authority includes the authority to enforce any provisions of the franchise for services, facilities, or equipment proposed by the cable operator which relate to *public*, educational, or governmental use of channel capacity, whether or not required by the franchising authority pursuant to subsection (b).

(d) In the case of any franchise under which channel capacity is designated under subsection (b), the franchising authority shall prescribe—

(1) rules and procedures under which the cable operator is permitted to use such channel capacity for the provision of other services if such channel capacity is not being used for the purposes designated, and

(2) rules and procedures under which such permitted use shall cease.

(e) Subject to section 624(d), a cable operator shall not exercise any editorial control over any *public*, educational, or governmental use of channel capacity provided pursuant to this section, except a cable operator may refuse to transmit any *public* access program or portion of a *public* access program which contains obscenity, indecency, or nudity.

(f) For purposes of this section, the term "institutional network" means a communication network which is constructed or operated by the cable operator and which is generally available only to subscribers who are not residential subscribers.

SEC. 532. Cable channels for commercial use

(a) Purpose

The purpose of this section is to promote competition in the delivery of diverse sources of video programming and to assure that the widest possible diversity of information sources are made available to the public from cable systems in a manner consistent with growth and development of cable systems.

(b) Designation of channel capacity for commercial use

(1) A cable operator shall designate channel capacity for commercial use by persons unaffiliated with the operator in accordance with the following requirements:

(A) An operator of any cable system with 36 or more (but not more than 54) activated channels shall designate 10 percent of such channels which are not otherwise required for use (or the use of which is not prohibited) by Federal law or regulation.

(B) An operator of any cable system with 55 or more (but not more than 100) activated channels shall designate 15 percent of such channels which are not otherwise required for use (or the use of which is not prohibited) by Federal law or regulation.

(C) An operator of any cable system with more than 100 activated channels shall designate 15 percent of all such channels.

(D) An operator of any cable system with fewer than 36 activated channels shall not be required to designate channel capacity for commercial use by persons unaffiliated with the operator, unless the cable system is required to provide such channel capacity under the terms of a franchise in effect on October 30, 1984.

(E) An operator of any cable system in operation on October 30, 1984, shall not be required to remove any service actually being provided on July 1, 1984, in order to comply with this section, but shall make channel capacity available for commercial use as such capacity becomes available until such time as the cable operator is in full compliance with this section.

(2) Any Federal agency, State, or franchising authority may not require any cable system to designate channel capacity for commercial use by unaffiliated persons in excess of the capacity specified in paragraph (1), except as otherwise provided in this section.

(3) A cable operator may not be required, as part of a request for proposals or as part of a proposal for renewal, subject to section 546 of this title, to designate channel capacity for any use (other than commercial use by unaffiliated persons under this section) except as provided in sections 531 and 557 of this title, but a cable operator may offer in a franchise, or proposal for renewal thereof, to provide, consistent with applicable law, such capacity for other than commercial use by such persons.

(4) A cable operator may use any unused channel capacity designated pursuant to this section until the use of such channel capacity is obtained, pursuant to a written agreement, by a person unaffiliated with the operator.

(5) For the purposes of this section, the term "commercial use" means the provision of video programming, whether or not for profit.

(6) Any channel capacity which has been designated for *public*, educational, or governmental use may not be considered as designated under this section for commercial use for purpose of this section.

(c) Use of channel capacity by unaffiliated persons; editorial control; restriction on service; rules on rates, terms, and conditions

(1) If a person unaffiliated with the cable operator seeks to use channel capacity designated pursuant to subsection (b) of this section for commercial use, the cable operator shall establish, consistent with the purpose of this section and with rules prescribed by the Commission under paragraph (4), the price, terms, and conditions of such use which are at least sufficient to assure that such use will not adversely affect the operation, financial condition, or market development of the cable system. (2) A cable operator shall not exercise any editorial control over any video programming provided pursuant to this section, or in any other way consider the content of such programming, except that a cable operator may refuse to transmit any leased access program or portion of a leased access program which contains obscenity, indecency, or nudity and may consider such content to the minimum extent necessary to establish a reasonable price for the commercial use of designated channel capacity by an unaffiliated person.

SEC. 534 (2) Use of *public*, educational, or governmental channels

A cable operator required to carry more than one signal of a qualified low power station under this subsection may do so, subject to approval by the franchising authority pursuant to section 531 of this title, by placing such additional station on *public*, educational, or governmental channels not in use for their designated purposes.

(d) Remedies

(1) Complaints by broadcast stations

Whenever a local commercial television station believes that a cable operator has failed to meet its obligations under this section, such station shall notify the operator, in writing, of the alleged failure and identify its reasons for believing that the cable operator is obligated to carry the signal of such station or has otherwise failed to comply with the channel positioning or repositioning or other requirements of this section. The cable operator shall, within 30 days of such written notification, respond in writing to such notification and either commence to carry the signal of such station in accordance with the terms requested or state its reasons for believing that it is not obligated to carry such signal or is in compliance with the channel positioning and repositioning and other requirements of this section. A local commercial television station that is denied carriage or channel positioning or repositioning in accordance with this section by a cable operator may obtain review of such denial by filing a complaint with the Commission. Such complaint shall allege the manner in which such cable operator has failed to meet its obligations and the basis for such allegations.

(2) Opportunity to respond

The Commission shall afford such cable operator an opportunity to present data and arguments to establish that there has been no failure to meet its obligations under this section.

(3) Remedial actions; dismissal

Within 120 days after the date a complaint is filed, the Commission shall determine whether the cable operator has met its obligations under this section. If the Commission determines that the cable operator has failed to meet such obligations, the Commission shall order the cable operator to reposition the complaining station or, in the case of an obligation to carry a station, to commence carriage of the station and to continue such carriage for at least 12 months. If the Commission determines that the cable operator has fully met the requirements of this section, it shall dismiss the complaint.

SEC. 535 (d) Placement of additional signals

A cable operator required to add the signals of qualified local noncommercial educational television stations to a cable system under this section may do so, subject to approval by the franchising authority pursuant to section 531 of this title, by placing such additional stations on *public*, educational, or governmental channels not in use for their designated purposes.

SEC. 541. General franchise requirements

(a) Authority to award franchises; public rights-of-way and easements; equal access to service; time for provision of service; assurances

(4) In awarding a franchise, the franchising authority—

(A) shall allow the applicant's cable system a reasonable period of time to become capable of providing cable service to all households in the franchise area;

(B) may require adequate assurance that the cable operator will provide adequate *public*, educational, and governmental access channel capacity, facilities, or financial support; and

(C) may require adequate assurance that the cable operator has the financial, technical, or legal qualifications to provide cable service.

SEC. 542. Franchise fees

(a) Payment under terms of franchise

Subject to the limitation of subsection (b) of this section, any cable operator may be required under the terms of any franchise to pay a franchise fee.

(b) Amount of fees per annum

For any twelve-month period, the franchise fees paid by a cable operator with respect to any cable system shall not exceed 5 percent of such cable operator's gross revenues derived in such period from the operation of the cable system to provide cable services. For purposes of this section, the 12-month period shall be the 12-month period applicable under the franchise for accounting purposes. Nothing in this subsection shall prohibit a franchising authority and a cable operator from agreeing that franchise fees which lawfully could be collected for any such 12-month period shall be paid on a prepaid or deferred basis; except that the sum of the fees paid during the term of the franchise may not exceed the amount, including the time value of money, which would have lawfully been collected if such fees had been paid per annum.

(c) Itemization of subscriber bills

Each cable operator may identify, consistent with the regulations prescribed by the Commission pursuant to section 543 of this title, as a separate line item on each regular bill of each subscriber, each of the following:

(1) The amount of the total bill assessed as a franchise fee and the identity of the franchising authority to which the fee is paid.

(2) The amount of the total bill assessed to satisfy any requirements imposed on the cable operator by the franchise agreement to support *public*, educational, or governmental channels or the use of such channels.

(3) The amount of any other fee, tax, assessment, or charge of any kind imposed by any governmental authority on the transaction between the operator and the subscriber.

(d) Court actions; reflection of costs in rate structures

In any court action under subsection (c) of this section, the franchising authority shall demonstrate that the rate structure reflects all costs of the franchise fees.

(e) Decreases passed through to subscribers

Any cable operator shall pass through to subscribers the amount of any decrease in a franchise fee.

(f) Itemization of franchise fee in bill

A cable operator may designate that portion of a subscriber's bill attributable to the franchise fee as a separate item on the bill.

(g) "Franchise fee" defined

For the purposes of this section—

(1) the term "franchise fee" includes any tax, fee, or assessment of any kind imposed by a franchising authority or other governmental entity on a cable operator or cable subscriber, or both, solely because of their status as such;

(2) the term "franchise fee" does not include—

(A) any tax, fee, or assessment of general applicability (including any such tax, fee, or assessment imposed on both utilities and cable operators or their services but not including a tax, fee, or assessment which is unduly discriminatory against cable operators or cable subscribers);

(B) in the case of any franchise in effect on October 30, 1984, payments which are required by the franchise to be made by the cable operator during the term of such franchise for, or in support of the use of, *public*, educational, or governmental access facilities;

(C) in the case of any franchise granted after October 30, 1984, capital costs which are required by the franchise to be incurred by the cable operator for *public*, educational, or governmental access facilities;

(D) requirements or charges incidental to the awarding or enforcing of the franchise, including payments for bonds, security funds, letters of credit, insurance, indemnification, penalties, or liquidated damages; or

(E) any fee imposed under title 17.

(h) Uncompensated services; taxes, fees and other assessments; limitation on fees

(1) Nothing in this chapter shall be construed to limit any authority of a franchising authority to impose a tax, fee, or other assessment of any kind on any person (other than a cable operator) with respect to cable service or other communications service provided by such person over a cable system for which charges are assessed to subscribers but not received by the cable operator.

(2) For any 12-month period, the fees paid by such person with respect to any such cable service or other communications service shall not exceed 5 percent of such person's gross revenues derived in such period from the provision of such service over the cable system.

(i) Regulatory authority of Federal agencies

Any Federal agency may not regulate the amount of the franchise fees paid by a cable operator, or regulate the use of funds derived from such fees, except as provided in this section.—

SEC. 543 (b) Establishment of basic service tier rate regulations

(1) Commission obligation to subscribers

The Commission shall, by regulation, ensure that the rates for the basic service tier are reasonable. Such regulations shall be designed to achieve the goal of protecting subscribers of any cable system that is not subject to effective competition from rates for the basic service tier that exceed the rates that would be charged for the basic service tier if such cable system were subject to effective competition.

(2) Commission regulations

Within 180 days after October 5, 1992, the Commission shall prescribe, and periodically thereafter revise, regulations to carry out its obligations under paragraph (1). In prescribing such regulations, the Commission—

(A) shall seek to reduce the administrative burdens on subscribers, cable operators, franchising authorities, and the Commission;

(B) may adopt formulas or other mechanisms and procedures in complying with the requirements of subparagraph (A); and

(C) shall take into account the following factors:

(i) the rates for cable systems, if any, that are subject to effective competition;

(ii) the direct costs (if any) of obtaining, transmitting, and otherwise providing signals carried on the basic service tier, including signals and services carried on the basic service tier pursuant to paragraph (7)(B), and changes in such costs;

(iii) only such portion of the joint and common costs (if any) of obtaining, transmitting, and otherwise providing such signals as is determined, in accordance with regulations prescribed by the Commission, to be reasonably and properly allocable to the basic service tier, and changes in such costs;

(iv) the revenues (if any) received by a cable operator from advertising from programming that is carried as part of the basic service tier or from other consideration obtained in connection with the basic service tier;

(v) the reasonably and properly allocable portion of any amount assessed as a franchise fee, tax, or charge of any kind imposed by any State or local authority on the transactions between cable operators and cable subscribers or any other fee, tax, or assessment of general applicability imposed by a governmental entity applied against cable operators or cable subscribers;

(vi) any amount required, in accordance with paragraph (4), to satisfy franchise requirements to support *public*, educational, or governmental channels or the use of such channels or any other services required under the franchise; and

(vii) a reasonable profit, as defined by the Commission consistent with the Commission's obligations to subscribers under paragraph (1).

(3) Equipment

The regulations prescribed by the Commission under this subsection shall include standards to establish, on the basis of actual cost, the price or rate for—

(A) installation and lease of the equipment used by subscribers to receive the basic service tier, including a converter box and a remote control unit and, if requested by the subscriber, such addressable converter box or other equipment as is required to access programming described in paragraph (8); and

(B) installation and monthly use of connections for additional television receivers.

(4) Costs of franchise requirements

The regulations prescribed by the Commission under this subsection shall include standards to identify costs attributable to satisfying franchise requirements to support *public*, educational, and governmental channels or the use of such channels or any other services required under the franchise.

(5) Implementation and enforcement

The regulations prescribed by the Commission under this subsection shall include additional standards, guidelines, and procedures concerning the implementation and enforcement of such regulations, which shall include—

(A) procedures by which cable operators may implement and franchising authorities may enforce the regulations prescribed by the Commission under this subsection;

(B) procedures for the expeditious resolution of disputes between cable operators and franchising authorities concerning the administration of such regulations;

(C) standards and procedures to prevent unreasonable charges for changes in the subscriber's selection of services or equipment subject to regulation under this section, which standards shall require that charges for changing the service tier selected shall be based on the cost of such change and shall not exceed nominal amounts when the system's configuration permits changes in service tier selection to be effected solely by coded entry on a computer terminal or by other similarly simple method; and

(D) standards and procedures to assure that subscribers receive notice of the availability of the basic service tier required under this section.

(6) Notice

The procedures prescribed by the Commission pursuant to paragraph (5)(A) shall require a cable operator to provide 30 days' advance notice to a franchising authority of any increase proposed in the price to be charged for the basic service tier.

(7) Components of basic tier subject to rate regulation

(A) Minimum contents

Each cable operator of a cable system shall provide its subscribers a separately available basic service tier to which subscription is required for access to any other tier of service. Such basic service tier shall, at a minimum, consist of the following:

(i) All signals carried in fulfillment of the requirements of sections 534 and 535 of this title.

(ii) Any public, educational, and governmental access programming required by the franchise of the cable system to be provided to subscribers.

(iii) Any signal of any television broadcast station that is provided by the cable operator to any subscriber, except a signal which is secondarily transmitted by a satellite carrier beyond the local service area of such station.

SEC. 545. Modification of franchise obligations

(a) Grounds for modification by franchising authority; public proceeding; time of decision

(1) During the period a franchise is in effect, the cable operator may obtain from the franchising authority modifications of the requirements in such franchise—

(A) in the case of any such requirement for facilities or equipment, including *public*, educational, or governmental access facilities or equipment, if the cable operator demonstrates that (i) it is commercially impracticable for the operator to comply with such requirement, and (ii) the proposal by the cable operator for modification of such requirement is appropriate because of commercial impracticability; or

(B) in the case of any such requirement for services, if the cable operator demonstrates that the mix, quality, and level of services required by the franchise at the time it was granted will be maintained after such modification.

(2) Any final decision by a franchising authority under this subsection shall be made in a public proceeding. Such decision shall be made within 120 days after receipt of such request by the franchising authority, unless such 120-day period is extended by mutual agreement of the cable operator and the franchising authority.

(b) Judicial proceedings; grounds for modification by court

(1) Any cable operator whose request for modification under subsection (a) of this section has been denied by a final decision of a franchising authority may obtain modification of such franchise requirements pursuant to the provisions of section 555 of this title.

(2) In the case of any proposed modification of a requirement for facilities or equipment, the court shall grant such modification only if the cable operator demonstrates to the court that:

(A) it is commercially impracticable for the operator to comply with such requirement; and

(B) the terms of the modification requested are appropriate because of commercial impracticability.

(3) In the case of any proposed modification of a requirement for services, the court shall grant such modification only if the cable operator demonstrates to the court that the mix, quality, and level of services required by the franchise at the time it was granted will be maintained after such modification.

(c) Rearrangement, replacement, or removal of service

Notwithstanding subsections (a) and (b) of this section, a cable operator may, upon 30 days' advance notice to the franchising authority, rearrange, replace, or remove a particular cable service required by the franchise if—

(1) such service is no longer available to the operator; or

(2) such service is available to the operator only upon the payment of a royalty required under section 801(b)(2) of title 17, which the cable operator can document—

(A) is substantially in excess of the amount of such payment required on the date of the operator's offer to provide such service, and

(B) has not been specifically compensated for through a rate increase or other adjustment.

(d) Rearrangement of particular services from one service tier to another or other offering of service

Notwithstanding subsections (a) and (b) of this section, a cable operator may take such actions to rearrange a particular service from one service tier to another, or otherwise offer the service, if the rates for all of the service tiers involved in such actions are not subject to regulation under section 543 of this title.

(e) Requirements for services relating to *public*, educational, or governmental access A cable operator may not obtain modification under this section of any requirement for services relating to public, educational, or governmental access.

(f) "Commercially impracticable" defined

For purposes of this section, the term "commercially impracticable" means, with respect to any requirement applicable to a cable operator, that it is commercially impracticable for the operator to comply with such requirement as a result of a change in conditions which is beyond the control of the operator and the nonoccurrence of which was a basic assumption on which the requirement was based.

SEC. 557. Existing franchises

(a) The provisions of—

(1) any franchise in effect on the effective date of this subchapter, including any such provisions which relate to the designation, use, or support for the use of channel capacity for *public*, educational, or governmental use, and

(2) any law of any State (as defined in section 153 of this title) in effect on October 30, 1984, or any regulation promulgated pursuant to such law, which relates to such designation, use or support of such channel capacity, shall remain in effect, subject to the express provisions of this subchapter, and for not longer than the then current remaining term of the franchise as such franchise existed on such effective date.

(b) For purposes of subsection (a) of this section and other provisions of this subchapter, a franchise shall be considered in effect on the effective date of this subchapter if such franchise was granted on or before such effective date.

SEC. 558. Criminal and civil liability

Nothing in this subchapter shall be deemed to affect the criminal or civil liability of cable programmers or cable operators pursuant to the Federal, State, or local law of libel, slander, obscenity, incitement, invasions of privacy, false or misleading advertising, or other similar laws, except that cable operators shall not incur any such liability for any program carried on any channel designated for *public*, educational, governmental use or on any other channel obtained under section 532 of this title or under similar arrangements unless the program involves obscene material.

Appendix 3

Table of Cited Law Cases

Pages	Case Name	Case Number	Date
17, 27, 144	U.S. v. O'Brien	391 U.S. 367	1968
18, 144	U.S. v. Southwestern Cable Co.	392 U.S. 157	1968
xx, xxv, 18, 141	Red Lion Broadcasting Co. v. FCC	395 U.S. 367	1969
xxiii, 20, 23,144	U.S. v. Midwest Video Corp. (Midwest Video I)	406 U.S. 649	1972
20, 139	Miami Herald Publishing Co. v. Tornillo	418 U.S. 241	1974
21, 127	American Civil Liberties Union v. FCC	523 F.2d 1344	1975
32, 129	Buckley v. Valeo	424 U.S. 1	1976
22, 140	National Association of Regulating Utility Commissioners v. FCC	533 F.2d 601	1976
22, 135	Home Box Office v. FCC	567 F.2d 9	1977
22, 129	Brookhaven Cable TV. v. Kelly	573 F.2d 765	1978
8, 23, 130, 132	FCC v. Midwest Video Corporation (Midwest II)	440 U.S. 689	1979
23, 130	Columbia Broadcasting System v. Democratic National Committee	412 U.S. 94	1973
23, 130	Community Communications v. City of Boulder	485 F.Supp. 1035	1980
24, 130	Community Television of Utah v. Roy City	555 F.Supp. 1164	1982
15, 33, 139	Missouri Knights of the Ku Klux Klan v. Kansas City, Missouri	723 F.Supp. 1347	1989
33, 140	Perry Education Association v. Perry Local Educators' Association	460 U.S. 37	1983
25, 44, 141	Rees v. State of Texas	909 S.W.2d	1995
25, 130, 134	Capital Cities Cable v. Crisp	467 U.S. 691	1984
26, 133, 141	Quincy Cable TV v. FCC	768 F.2d 1434	1985
15, 33, 128	Berkshire Cablevision of RI v. Burke	773 F.2d 382	1985
15, 27, 132	Erie Telecommunications v. City of Erie	659 F.Supp. 580	1987
33, 144	Turner Broadcasting System v. FCC	512 U.S. 1145	1994
33, 144	Turner Broadcasting System v. FCC	117 S.Ct. 1174	1997

Pages	Case Name	Case Number	Date
29, 127	Alliance for Community Media v. FCC	10 F.3d 812	1993
28, 33, 131	Daniels Cablevision v. U.S.	835 F.Supp. 1	1993
xxv, 29, 131	Denver Area Educational Telecommunications Consortium v. FCC	116 S.Ct. 2374	1996

Appendix 4

Special Resources

Alliance for Community Media
666 11th St. NW, Suite 806
Washington, DC 20001-4542
Phone: 202-393-2650
Fax: 202-393-2653
Jobline: 408-864-5413
E-mail: ALLIANCECM@AOL.COM
http://www.alliancecm.org

Free or At-Cost Programming

The Department of Education
Satellite Meeting Series
Can be downlinked on C-Band or Ku-Band
Phone: 800-USA-LEARN
E-mail: Satellite_Town_Meeting@ed.gov
http://www.ed.gov.inits/stm

The First Amendment Center at Vanderbilt University
1207 18th Avenue South
Nashville, TN 37212
Phone: 615-321-9588
E-mail: wholcomb@fac.org

Media Literacy Information

Center for Media Literacy
4727 Wilshire Blvd., Suite 403
Los Angeles, CA 90010

National Telemedia Council, Inc.
120 E. Wilson St.
Madison, WI 53703

Center for Media and Values
1962 S. Shenandoah St.
Los Angeles, CA 90034
Media Literacy Online Project
http://interact.uoregon.edu/MediaLit/HomePage

New Mexico Media Literacy Project
http://www.nmmlp.org/

Just Think Foundation
http://www.justthink.org

Center for Media Literacy
http://www.medialit.org

Nonprofit Information (Including Fund Raising)

Benton Foundation
1634 Eye Street NW, 12th Floor
Washington, DC 20006
Phone: 202-638-5770
Fax: 202-638-5771
E-mail: benton@benton.org
http://www.benton.org

Nonprofit Resource Center
An immense directory of Internet resources for nonprofits.
http://not-for-profit.org/index.html

Center for Nonprofit Management
University of St. Thomas
52 Tenth Street South
Minneapolis, MN 55403
Phone: 612-962-4290
Fax: 612-962-4810
Offers workshops and classes on advanced topics in fund raising.

The Foundation Center
79 Fifth Avenue
New York, NY 10003
Phone: 212-620-4230 or 800-424-9836
http://fndcenter.org
An independent nonprofit information clearinghouse.

National Center for Nonprofit Boards
2000 L Street, NW
Washington, DC 20036
Phone: 800-883-6262 or 202-452-6262
Fax: 202-452-6299
http://www.ncnb.org
Publications and other resources for board development and fund raising.

National Society of Fund-Raising Executives
1101 King Street, Suite 700
Alexandria, VA 22314
Phone: 703-684-0410
Fax: 703-684-0540
http://www.nsfre.org
A professional association for fund raisers.

Books

Klein, Kim. *Fundraising for Social Change*, 3d ed. Inverness, CA: Chardon Press, 1994.

Odendahl, Teresa. *Charity Begins at Home*. New York: NY Basic Books, Inc., 1990.
Poderis, Tony. *It's a Great Day to Fund Raise*. Willoughby Hills, OH: FundAmerica Press, 1996.
Seltzer, Michael. *Securing Your Organization's Future*. New York: The Foundation Center, 1987.
Shannon, James P., Ed. *The Corporate Contributions Handbook*. San Francisco: Jossey-Bass Inc., 1991.

Other Publications

The Chronicle of Philanthropy
published biweekly
1255 23rd Street, NW
Washington, DC 20037

Philanthropy Journal Online
http://www.philanthropy-journal.org
Daily on-line news service from Philanthropy News Network.

Nonprofit World: The National Nonprofit Leadership and Management Journal
published monthly
Society for Nonprofit Organizations
6314 Odana Road, Suite 1
Madison, WI 53719
Phone: 800-424-7367
Other Resources

Grassroots Fundraising Series, a seven-part video series featuring trainer Kim Klein.
122 West Franklin Avenue, Suite 518
Minneapolis, MN 55404
Phone: 612-879-0602
A video dealing with the special fund raising needs of grassroots organizations.

Headwaters Fund
Grants and Related Resources
http://www.lib.msu.edu/harris23/grants/maillist.htm
Mailing Lists and Discussion Forum lists that fund raisers can subscribe to.

Fundsnet
http://www.fundsnetservices.com
A comprehensive directory of Internet resources about fund raising and grant writing.

InnoNet Toolbox
http://www.inetwork.org/prog.html
Detailed information about fund raising plans, program plans, and evaluation plans.

References

The ABC's of Fund Seeking. Washington, DC: American Association of Retired Persons, 1994. *Abrams, et al. v. United States*, 250 U.S. 616 (1919).

"Access Channel Program Content Sparks Controversy." *The News Media and The Law* (summer 1991): 21–22.

Advertising by Charities: A Practical Guide to Raising Money by Press Advertising, Direct Mail, Posters, Radio and Television Appeals and Telephone Selling. London: Directory of Social Change, 1986.

Alexander, Ron, and Ira Gallen. "Past Creates Wave of TV Nostalgia." *New York Times*, 2 August 1990, Final edition, sec. C, p. 1.

Allard, Nicholas W. "1992 Cable Act: Just the Beginning." *Hastings Comm/Ent Law Journal* 15 (1993): 305–55.

Allen, Robert C. *Channels of Discourse, Reassembled*. Chapel Hill: University of North Carolina Press, 1992.

"Alliance for Community Media Takes Case to Supreme Court." *Manhattan Neighborhood Network News* 1, no. 3 (1995): 1–2.

Alliance for Community Media v. Federal Communications Commission, 10 F.3d 812 (D.C. Cir. 1993).

Alternative Revenue Sources: Prospects, Requirements and Concerns for Nonprofits. San Francisco: Jossey-Bass, 1996.

Alvarez, Sally. "Television for the People." *News and Record* (Greensboro, North Carolina) 4 September 1994: sec. A, p. 6.

Alvarez, Sally. "Reclaiming the Public Sphere: A Study of Public Access Cable Television Programming by the United States Labor Movement." Ph.D. Dissertation. Unpublished. Emory University (Atlanta, GA): 1995.

Alvarez, Sally. "Building Community Support." *Community Media Review* (Spring 1997): 9, 20–21.

American Civil Liberties Union v. Federal Communications Commission, 523 F.2d 1344 (1975).

Ammon, Ann, and Randal L. Sheeham. "National Issues Forum: The Reading and Pocatello Experiences." *Community Television Review* 9, no. 1 (1986): 24–25.

Amos, Janell Shride. *Fundraising Ideas: Over 225 Money Making Events for Community Groups*. Jefferson, North Carolina: McFarland, 1995.

Aristotle. *Rhetoric*. Translated by W. Rhys Roberts. New York: Random House, 1954.

Aristotle. *The Politics*. Ed. Stephen Everson. Cambridge, England: University of Cambridge Press, 1988.

Aspen's Guide to 60 Successful Special Events: How to Plan, Organize and Conduct Outstanding Fund Raisers. Gaithersburg, MD: Aspen Public, 1996.

Atkin, David, and Robert LaRose. "Cable Access: Market Concerns Amidst the Marketplaces of Ideas." *Journalism Quarterly* 68 (Fall 1991): 354–62.

Aufderheide, Pat. "150 Channels and Nothin' On." *The Progressive* 56 (1992): 36–38.

Aufderheide, Pat. "Cable Television and the Public Interest." *Journal of Communication* 42 (Winter 1992): 52–65.

Aufderheide, Patricia. "Underground Cable: A Survey of Public Access Programming." *Afterimage* (Summer 1994): 5–8.

Aufderheide, Pat, and Jeffrey Chester. *Talk Radio: Who's Talking? Who's Listening?* Washington, DC: Benton Foundation, 1990.

Bagdikian, Ben H. *The Media Monopoly*. 4th ed. Boston: Beacon Press, 1992.

Baker, Bob. "'Poker Party's' Freewheeling Ace." *Los Angeles Times*, 27 October 1992, Home edition, sec. F, p. 9.

Barendt, Eric. "Access to Broadcasting." In *Broadcasting Law: A Comparative Study*. Oxford: Oxford University Press, 1993.

Barendt, Eric. "New Mind the Ownership, What About the Quality." *Index on Censorship* (April/May 1994): 224–27.

Barnouw, Eric. *Tube of Plenty: The Evolution of American Television*. New York: Oxford University Press, 1977.

Barron, James. "Cable TV: The Big Picture." New York Times, 10 April 1994, p. 14.

Bauer, David G. *The "How-To" Grants Manual: Successful Grantseeking Techniques for Obtaining Public and Private Grants*. 3d ed. Phoenix: Oryx Press, 1995.

Bauer, David G. *The Effective Grantwriter*. Lincoln, NE: University of Nebraska Television, 1992.

Beck, Kirsten. *Cultivating the Wasteland: Can Cable Put the Vision back in Television?* New York: American Council for the Arts, 1983.

Becker, Carl L. *Freedom and Responsibility in the American Way of Life*. New York: Alfred A. Knopf, 1945.

Beecher, Andy. "Government Corner: James City County Government Access: Sacramento County Election Coverage." *Community Television Review* 9, no. 4 (1986): 20–21.

Bell, Jim. "Programming for Citizens: A Different Kind of Television." *Public Management* (June 1980): 5–7.

Bergin, Bonita M. "Assessing Cost, Risks and Results." In *Achieving Excellence in Fund Raising*. Ed. by Henry A. Rosso. San Francisco: Jossey-Bass, 1991.

Berkshire Cablevision v. Burke, 659 F.Supp. 580 (W.D. Pa. 1987).

Bernet, Mark J. "Quincy Cable and Its Effect on Access Provisions of the 1984 Cable Act." *Notre Dame Law Review* 61 (1986): 426–39.

Bernstein, Andrew A. "Access to Cable, Natural Monopoly and the First Amendment." *Columbia Law Review* 86 (1986): 1663–96.

Blasius, Chip. *Earning More Funds: Effective, Proven Fund Raising Strategies for Youth Groups*. Fort Wayne, IN: B.C. Creations, 1992.

Blau, Andrew. "Can We Talk? Access, Democracy and Connecting the Disconnected." Portland, OR: National Federation of Local Cable Programmers Convention, July 1991. Photocopied.

Blau, Andrew. "The Promise of Access." *The Independent* (April 1992): 22–26.

Blau, Andrew. "Soapbox Among the Soaps." *Index on Censorship* (February 1993): 5–7+.

Bloland, Harland G., and Rita Bornstein. "Fund Raising in Transition: Strategies for Professionalization." In *Taking Fund Raising Seriously*. Ed. by Dwight R. Burlingame and Lamont J. Hulse. San Francisco: Jossey-Bass, 1991.

Bluem, A. William. *Documentary in American Television*. New York: Hastings House, 1979.

Blum, Laurie. *The Complete Guide to Getting a Grant: How to Turn Your Ideas into Dollars*. New York: John Wiley & Sons, 1996.

Bogart, Lee. "Shaping a New Media Policy." *The Nation* (12 July 1993): 57–60.

Bollier, David. *The Information Superhighway and the Reinvention of Television*. Washington, DC: Center for Media Education, 1993.

Boozell, Greg, "What's Wrong with Public access Television?" *Art Papers* 17, no. 4 (July/August 1993): 7.

Boudreaux, Donald J., and Robert B. Ekelund, Jr. "The Cable Television Consumer Protection and Competition Act of 1992: The Triumph of Private over Public Interest." *Alabama Law Review* 44 (1993): 355–91.

Breiteneicher, Joe. *Quest for Funds Revisited: A Fund-Raising Starter Kit*. Washington, DC: National Trust for Historic Preservation, 1993.

Brenner, Daniel L., and Monroe E. Price. "The 1984 Cable Act: Prologue and Precedents." *Cardozo Arts and Entertainment* 4 (1985): 19–50.

Bretz, Rudy. "Public Access Cable Television: Audiences." *Journal of Communication* (summer 1975): 23–32.

Brey, Andy. "Instructional Television: Meeting the Needs of the Adult Learner." *Community Television Review* 8, no. 4 (1985): 28–29.

Briller, Bert. "Accent on Access Television." *Television Quarterly* 28, no. 2 (Spring 1996): 51–58.

Broadcasting and Cable Yearbook 1998. New Providence, NJ: R. R. Bowker, 1998.

Brody, Leslie G. *Effective Fund Raising: Tools and Techniques for Success*. Acton, MA: Copley Publishing Group, 1994.

Brody, Ralph. *Fund Raising Events: Strategies for Success*. Cleveland, OH: Federation for Community Planning, 1993.

Brookhaven Cable TV, Inc. v. Kelly, 573 F.2d 765 (1979).

Brown, Les. "Free Expression is Unwelcome Rider of the Runaway Technology Train." Paper presented at the annual convention of the National Federation of Local Cable Programmers Convention, July 1980. Photocopied.

Buckley v. Valeo, 424 US 1 (1976).

Bunker, Matthew D. "Levels of First Amendment Scrutiny and Cable Access Channel Requirements." *Communication and Law* 15 (1993): 3–20.

Burlingame, Dwight. "Raising Money for Public Libraries: Insights from Experience." *New Directions for Philanthropic Fundraising* (fall 1995): 95–107.

Buske, Sue Miller. "Improving Local Community Access Programming." *Public Management* 62, no. 5 (June 1980): 12–14.

Buske, Sue, and Dirk Koning. "Public, Educational and Governmental Access: Issues and Answers." *Community Television Review* 5 (Spring 1991): 5.

"Cable and the Public." *Greensboro (North Carolina) Daily News*, 12 April 1979, sec. A, p. 4.

Cable Communications Policy Act of 1984, U.S. Code, vol 47, sec. 531–559, 611 (1984).

Cable Television Consumer Protection and Competition Act of 1992, U.S. Code, vol. 47, sec. 531–59 (1992).

"Cable Television Information Bulletin." *Federal Communications Commission Fact Sheet* (November 1996): 1–26.

"Cable Television in North Carolina." Raleigh, NC: N.C. Center for Public Policy Research, Inc., (1978): 30–45.

Cable Television Report and Order 36 FCC 2d 143 (1972).

Cahill, Sheila M. "The Public Forum: Minimum Access, Equal Access and the First Amendment." *Stanford Law Review* 28 (November 1975): 117–148.

Capital Cities Cable v. Crisp, 467 US 2694 (1984).

Caristi, D. *Expanding Free Expression in the Marketplace: Broadcasting and the Public Forum*. Westport, CT: Quorum Books, 1992.

Cavin, Winston. "City Council Blasts 'Sorry' Cable TV," *Greensboro (North Carolina) Daily News*, 7 March 1979, sec. B, p. 1, 9.

"Censored Air." *The Nation* 253, no. 2 (July/August 1991): 39–40.

Century Communications v. Federal Communications Commission, 835 F.2d 292 (D.C. Cir. 1987).

Cerone, Daniel. "Time Warner Group Takes Big Step toward Future of Cable Television." *News & Record* (Greensboro, NC), 21 December 1991, sec. A, p. 22.

Charities and Broadcasting: A Guide to Radio and Television Appeals and Grants. London: Directory of Social Change, 1988.

Chess, Harvey. *Resources for Your Nonprofit Organization: A How To Do it Handbook*. Los Angeles: California Community Foundation, 1993.

Chun, Réne. "Here's Joey!" *New York* 31, no. 18 (11 May 1998): 32–37.

Church, Laurel M. "Community Access Television: What We Don't Know and Why We Don't Know It." *Journal of Film and Video* 39 (Summer 1987): 6–13.

City of Greensboro Cable Task Force Report, City of Greensboro, NC, September 1992. Unpublished.

Civille, Brian. "The Internet and the Poor." In *Public Access to the Internet*. Ed. Brian Kahlin and James Keller, 176–207. Cambridge, MA: MIT Press, 1995.

Clark, Jim. "Revolt in Videoland," *Triad (North Carolina)* 4, no. 1 (Winter 1979): 17–21.

Clarkson, Robert L. "Invalidation of Mandatory Cable Access Requirements: Federal Communications Commission v. Midwest Video Corporation." *Pepperdine Law Review* 7 (1980): 469–89.

Clement, Hayes. "Students Learn about Television and Real Life." *News and Record* (Greensboro, NC) 26 July 1990, sec. People and Places, p. 1.

Cnaan, Ram, and Felice Perlmutter. "Using Private Money to Finance Public Services: The Case of the Philadelphia Department of Recreation." *New Directions for Philanthropic Fundraising* (Fall 1995): 53–73.

Communication Act of 1934, U.S. Code, sec. 47.

Columbia Broadcasting System, Inc. v. Democratic National Committee, 412 US 94 (1973).

Community Channels, Free Speech & the Law: A Layman's Guide to Access Programming on Cable Television. San Francisco: Foundation for Community Service, 1988.

Community Communications Company v. City of Boulder, 485 F.Supp. 1035 (1980).

Community Media Resource Directory, Washington, DC: Alliance for Community Media, 1994

Community Television of Utah v. Roy City, 555 F.Supp. 1164 (1982).

Connelly, Anne. *Going—Going—Gone!: Successful Auctions for Non-Profit Institutions.* Greenwich, CT: Target Funding Group, 1993.

Cooke, Kevin, and Dan Lehrer. "The Whole World is Talking." *The Nation* (12 July 1993): 60–64.

Copelan, John Journal, Jr., and A. Quinn Jones, III. "Cable Television, Public Access and Local Governments." *Entertainment and Sports Law Journal* 1 (1984): 37–51.

Corson, Ross. "Cable's Missed Connection: A Revolution that Won't Be Televised." In *American Mass Media: Industries & Issues.* Ed. Robert Atwan, Barry Orton, and William Vesterman. New York: Random House, 1986.

Coustel, J. P. "New Rules for Cable Television in the United States: Reducing the Market Power of Cable Operators." *Telecommunications Policy* (April 1993): 200–20.

Cumerford, William R. *Start-to-Finish Fund Raising: How a Professional Organizes and Conducts a Successful Campaign.* Chicago: Precept Press, 1993.

Curran, James. "Mass Media and Democracy: A Reappraisal." In *Mass Media and Society.* Ed. James Curran and Michael Gurevitch, 82–117. New York: Edward Arnold, 1991.

Cutlip, Scott M. "Fund Raising in the U.S." *Society* 27 (March/April 1990): 59–62.

Czuckrey, William N. *Games for Fundraising.* Sarasota, FL: Pineapple Press, 1995.

Dager, Donna. "Providing Public Access to Children." *Community Television Review* 8, no. 4 (1985): 12–15.

Dahlgren, Peter. *Television and the Public Sphere: Citizenship, Democracy and the Media.* London: Sage Publications, 1995.

Daley, Beth. "Tuning in Community TV." *Boston Sunday Globe*, 11 February 1996, NorthWeekly, p. 1, 20.

Daniels Cablevision, Inc. v. United States, 835 F.Supp. 1 (D.D.C. 1993).

Deetz, Stanley A. *Democracy in an Age of Corporate Colonization.* Albany, New York: SUNY Press, 1992.

Denver Area Educational Telecommunications Consortium v. Federal Communications Commission, 116 S.Ct. 2374 (1996).

Detroit, Doyle. Westsound Community Access Television, Bremerton, Washington, <DDetroit@aol.com>, Alliance for Community Media Listserv (a national, on-line newsgroup for public access workers, supporters, and advocates), 29 March 1997, 1:06 PM.

Devine, Robert H. "Protecting the Diversity." *Community Television Review* 9, no. 1 (1986): 34–35.

Devine, Robert H. "Video, Access and Agency." St. Paul, MN: National Federation of Local Cable Programmers Convention, 17 July 1992. Photocopied.

Devine, Robert H. "Discourses on Access: The Marginalization of a Medium." San Antonio, TX: Speech Communication Association Convention, November 1995. Photocopied.

Devine, Robert H. "Citizenship or Consumership." *Community Media Review* 19, no. 3 (1996): 9.

DeWitt, Clyde. "Obscenity Law: What Does it Mean? . . . And Is it Fair?" *Community Television Review* (November/December 1991): 12.

Dillon, Paul. "Activist Urges County to Rethink Public-Access TV." *Orlando Business Journal*, 15 (28 August-3 September 1998): 3, 62.

Discover Total Resources: A Guide for Nonprofits. Pittsburgh, PA: Mellon Bank Corp., 1995.

Dority, Barbara. "Taking the Public Access out of Public Access." *The Humanist* 54, no. 6 (November 1994): 37.

Doty, Pamela. "Public Access Cable Television: Who Cares?" *Journal of Communication* 25, (Summer 1975): 33–41.

Doyle, William. *Fund Raising 101: How to Raise Money for Charities.* Kingsport, TN: American Fund Raising Institute, 1993.

Doyle, William L. *Fund Raising Ideas for All Nonprofits: Charities, Churches, Clubs, etc.* Kingsport, TN: American Fund Raising Institute, 1995.

"Educational Access the Leader in Lubbock." *Community Television Review* (spring 1991): 9–10.

Elischer, Tony. *Fund Raising.* London: Hodder and Stoughton, 1995.

Emerson, Thomas. *The System of Freedom of Expression.* New York: Random House, 1970.

Engelman, Ralph, "The Origins of Public Access Cable Television 1966-1972." *Journalism Monographs.* 23 (October 1990): 1–47.

Engelman, Ralph. *Public Radio and Television in America: A Political History.* Thousand Oaks, CA: Sage Publications, 1996.

Entman, Robert. *Democracy without Citizens.* New York: Oxford University Press, 1989.

Entman, Robert M., and Steven S. Wildman. "Reconciling Economic and Non-Economic Perspectives on Media Policy: Transcending the Marketplace of Ideas." *Journal of Communication* (Winter 1992): 5–19.

Erie Telecommunications v. City of Erie, 723 F.Supp. 1347 (W.D. Mo. 1989).

Espinoza, Rick. *The Carnival Handbook and Other Fundraising Ideas!* Los Angeles, CA: Century West, 1994.

Evans, S. M., and H. Boyte. *Free Spaces: The Sources of Democratic Change in America.* New York: Harper and Row, 1986.

Events and Fund-Raisers: Hundreds of Copyright-Free Illustrations—All Ready to Use! Cincinnati, OH: F&W Publications, 1995.

Farhi, Paul. "Keeping an Eye on Cable Television." *Washington Post National Weekly Edition*, 10–16 February 1992, p. 6–7.

Federal Communications Commission v. Midwest Video Corporation, 440 US 689 (1979).

Ferguson, Majorie. *Public Communication: The New Imperatives.* London: SAGE Publications, 1990.

Ferguson, Jacqueline. *The Grant Organizer: A Streamlined System for Seeking, Winning and Managing Grants.* Alexandria, VA: Capitol Publications, 1993.

Ferguson, Jacqueline. *The Grants Development Kit.* Alexandria, VA: Capitol, 1993.

Ferguson, Jacqueline. *The Grantseeker's Answer Book: Grants Experts Respond to the Most Commonly Asked Questions.* Alexandria, VA: Capitol, 1995.

Fey, Don. *The Complete Book of Fund-Raising Writing.* Rosemont, NJ: Morris-Lee Publishing Group, 1995.

Financial Practices for Effective Fundraising. San Francisco: Jossey-Bass, 1994.

Finnegan, John R., Sr., and Claudia A. Haskel. "America and the Bill of Rights at a Historical Crossroads." *Community Television Review* (November/December 1991): 7.

First Report and Order, 38 FCC 683 (1965).

Flanagan, Joan. *The Grass Roots Fundraising Book: How to Raise Money in Your Community.* Chicago: Contemporary Books, 1995.

Fogal, Robert E. "Standards and Ethics in Fundraising." In *Achieving Excellence in Fund Raising.* Ed. Henry A. Rosso. San Francisco: Jossey-Bass, 1991.

Fortnightly Corp. v. United Artists Television, 392 US 390 (1968).

The Foundation Center's User-Friendly Guide: Grantseeker's Guide to Resources. Rev. ed. New York: The Foundation Center, 1996.

Fowler, Deborah L. "Diverse Programming v. Community Standards: The Constituionality of Municipal Censorship of Leased Access Cable." *San Diego Law Review* 27 (1990): 493–519.

"Foxborough Council for Human Services." *Benton Bulletin* 3 (1990):

A Free and Responsible Press: A General Report on Mass Communication, Commission on Freedom of the Press. Chicago: University of Chicago Press, 1947.

From Here to Technology: How to Fund Hardware, Software, and More. Arlington, Virginia: American Association of School Administrators, 1995.

Fuller, Linda K. *Community Television in the United States: A Sourcebook on Public, Educational, and Governmental Access.* Westport, CT: Greenwood Press, 1994.

Funding Resources Guide: 1996–97. Madison, WI: Associated Students of Madison, 1996.

Funding Sources for Community and Economic Development: A Guide to Current Sources for Local Programs and Projects. Phoenix, AZ: Oryx Press, 1995.

Fundraising by Public Institutions. San Francisco: Jossey-Bass, 1995.

Fund Raising Effectiveness: A Manual of Systems and Procedures for Higher Fundraising Productivity. New York: Nonprofit Management Group, CUNY, 1992.

Gaffney, Michael D. "Quincy Cable Television, Inc. v. Federal Communications Commission: Judicial Deregulation of Cable Television via the First Amendment." *Suffolk University Law Review* 20 (1986): 1179–1202.

Garnham, Nicholas. "The Media and the Public Sphere." *Intermedia* (January 1986): 28–33.

Garrett, Laurel L. F. "Public Access Channels in Cable Television: The Economic Scarcity Rationale of Berkshire v. Burke." *Kentucky Law Journal* 74 (1986): 249–67.

Geller, Henry, and Donna Lampert. "Cable, Content Regulation and the First Amendment." *Catholic University Law Review* 32 (1983): 603–21.

George, Deborah. "The Cable Communications Policy Act of 1984 and Content Regulation of Cable Television." *New England Law Review* 20, no. 4 (1984–85): 779–804.

Getting $'s for Your Project. Woodhaven, NY: Queens Council on the Arts, 1994.

Gilbertson, Peggy M. "Building a Volunteer Crew." *Community Television Review* 9, no. 3 (1986): 6–7.

Gillespie, Andrew, and Kevin Robins. "Geographical Inequalities: The Spatial Bias of the New Communications Technologies." *Community Television Review* 16, no. 2 (March/April 1993): 18.

Gillespie, Gilbert. *Public Access Cable Television in the United States and Canada.* New York: Praeger, 1975.

Gilmore, Elizabeth. "Pikas or Dinosaurs?: The Story of a Museum Television Show." *Community Television Review* 10, no. 1 (1987): 30–31.

Glenn-Davitian, Lauren. "Building the Empire: Access as Community Animation." *Journal of Film and Video* 39 (Summer 1987): 35–39.

Glist, Paul. "Cable Must Carry—Again." *Federal Communications Law Journal* 39 (1987): 109–21.

Good, Leslie T. "Power, Hegemony and Communication Theory in Cultural Politics." In *Contemporary America.* Ed. Ian Angus and Sut Jhally. New York: Routledge, 1989.

"Good Samaritan Hospital and Medical Center." *Benton Bulletin* 3 (April 1990): 37–39.

Graber, Doris A. *Processing the News: How People Tame the Information Tide*. New York: Longman, 1984.

Graber, Doris A. *Mass Media and American Politics*. Washington, DC: CQ Press, 1993.

Grabiner, Liz. "Empowering Disadvantaged Students." *Community Television Review* 8, no. 4 (1985): 10–11.

Graham, Andrea. "Tampa Bay Performs." *Community Television Review* 10, no. 1 (1987): 12.

Grant$ for Film, Media and Communications. New York: The Center, 1985.

Grantseeker's Desk Reference. Greenville, SC: Polaris, 1994.

The Grantseeker's Handbook of Essential Internet Sites. Alexandria, VA: Capitol Publications, 1996.

Grant Seeking Fundamentals. Greenville, SC: Polaris, 1994.

GrantWrite: A Step-by-Step System for Writing Grant Proposals that Win. Alexandria, VA: Capitol Publications, 1993.

Grant Writer's Assistant. Woodstock, GA: Falling Rock Software, 1994.

Grassroots Fundraising. Sacramento, CA: California State Library, 1995.

Greenfield, James M. "Financial Practices for Effective Fundraising." *New Directions for Philanthropic Fundraising* (Spring 1994): 1–16.

Greenfield, Laura B. "Measuring Audiences For Government Access Programming." *Community Television Review* 8, no. 3 (1985): 8–9.

Gross, Charles. "Two on the Aisle: They're Public Access TV, Taking their Camcorder to Broadway Shows." *Camcorder* 13, no. 8 (August 1997): 94–98.

Gross, Jane. "Using Cable TV to Get Child Support. *New York Times*, 14 November 1993, Final edition, sec. 1, p. 20.

Gruson, Lindsey. "Cablevision to Post Bond, to Install Public Access," *Greensboro (North Carolina) Daily News*, 12 April 1979, sec. C, p. 1.

Guidelines for Fundraising: Step by Step Fundraising. St. Paul, MN: Minnesota Association of Library Friends, 1995.

Gullett, Pamela B. "The 1984 Cable Flip Flop: From *Capital Cities Cable, Inc. v. Crisp* to the Cable Communications Policy Act." *The American University Law Review* 34 (1985): 557–90.

Habermas, Jurgen. "The Public Sphere." In *Rethinking Popular Culture: Contemporary Perspectives in Cultural Studies*. Ed. Chandra Mukerji and Michael Schudson. Berkeley, CA: University of California Press, 1991.

Habermas, Jurgen. *The Structural Transformation of the Public Sphere*. Cambridge, MA: MIT Press, 1989.

Hagon, Roger. "The Electronic Classroom in Trempeleau County, Wisconsin." *Community Television Review* 8, no. 4 (1985): 16–17.

Halleck, Dee Dee. "Whittling Away at the Public Sphere." *Community Television Review* 16, no. 2 (March/April 1993): 14.

Hammer, John. "No Standards for Public Access Television." *The Rhinocerous Times*, 5 September 1996, p. 1.

Hardenbergh, Margaret B. "Promise versus Performance: A Case Study of Four Public Access Channels in Connecticut." Ph.D. diss., New York University, 1985.

Harmon, Mark D. "Hate Groups and Cable Public Access." *Journal of Mass Media Ethics* 6, no. 3 (1991): 146–55.

Harris, Scott. "They Watch their Television Religiously." *Los Angeles Times*, 2 May 1993, Valley edition, sec. B, p. 1.

Harris, Susan. "L.I. Cable Company Ordered to Restore a Public-Access Program." *New York Times*, 14 August 1994, Final edition, sec. 1, p. 44.

Harrison, Bill J. *Fundraising–The Good, the Bad, and the Ugly (and How to Tell the Difference): A Nuts and Bolts Approach to Successful Fundraising*. Phoenix, AZ: Oryx Press, 1996.

Hathaway, Maureen. "An Integrated Approach." *Public Management* (June 1980): 10–11.

Hayes, Rick. "Building First Amendment Partnerships." *Community Television Review* (November/December 1991): 14.

Hernandez, Raymond. "Albany on the Air: Politically Savvy and Cable-Ready," *New York Times*, 20 June 1996, sec. B, p. 1.

Herring, Mark R. "TCC and Five Years of the Cable Communications Policy Act of 1984: Tuning out the Consumer?" *University of Richmond Law Journal* 24, no. 127 (1989): 151–70.

Higgins, John M. "L.A. Mayor Rejects Public Access Funding." *Broadcasting & Cable* 128, no. 36 (31 August 1998): 47.

Hill, Chris. "Television Judit and Video Andras: An Interview with Judit Kopper and Andras Solyom." *The Humanist* (May/June 1994): 9–14.

Hill, Steven. "Speech May Be Free, but it Sure Isn't Cheap." *The Humanist* 54, no. 3 (May 1994): 6.

Hocking, William Ernest. *Freedom of the Press: A Framework of Principle*. Chicago: University of Chicago Press, 1972.

Hogan, Margaret Mullen. "Public Hospital Fundraising in an Era of Health Care Reform." *New Directions for Philanthropic Fundraising* (Fall 1995): 109–25.

Hollander, Richard. *Video Democracy*. Mt. Airy, MD: Lomond Publications, 1985.

Hollick, Clive. "Media Regulation and Democracy." *Index on Censorship* (April/May 1994): 54–58.

Hollinrake, John D., Jr. "Cable Television: Public Access and the First Amendment." *Communications and the Law* 9, no. 1 (February 1987): 3–40.

Home Box Office, Inc. v. Federal Communications Commission, 567 F.2d 9 (1977).

Hopkins, Karen Brooks. *Successful Fundraising for Arts and Cultural Organizations*. Phoenix, AZ: Oryx Press, 1996.

Hops, Jeffrey. "Federal Appeals Court Declares PEG Access, DBS Non-Profit Set Aside Constitutional." Alliance for Community Media *Public Policy Update*, 18 Sept. 1996, p. 1.

Horwood, James N. "Public, Educational, and Governmental Access on Cable Television: A Model to Assure Reasonable Access to the Information Superhighway for All People in Fulfillment of the First Amendment Guarantee of Free Speech." *Seton Hall Law Review* 25 (1995): 1413–45.

Horwood, James N. "Public Access and Internet: An Electronic Village of Voices." Raleigh, North Carolina: Alliance for Community Media Southeast and Mid-Atlantic Conference, November 1994. Photocopied.

How to Get More Grant$. Arlington, VA: Government Information Services, 1994.

How to Write a Winning Foundation Proposal. New York: Jean Sigler and Associates, 1994.

Howe, Fisher. *Fund Raising and the Nonprofit Board Member*. Washington, DC: National Center for Nonprofit Boards, 1990.

Howe, Fisher. *The Board Member's Guide to Fund Raising*. San Francisco: Jossey-Bass, 1991.

H. R. Rep No. 934, 98th Congress, 2nd Sess. 55, reprinted in *1984 U.S. Code Congressional and Administration News, 4655.*

Ingraham, Sharon B. "Access Channels: The Problem is Prejudice." *Multichannel News* 12, no. 37 (16 September 1991): 43.

"Investigating Talk-Radio as Political Discourse." *Newslink* 6, no. 3 (fall 1996): 10.

Iverem, Esther. "Public Access Programs Scheduled for Brooklyn." *Newsday* (4 July 1990): 29.

Jacobs, Andrew. "The Howard Stern of Cable." *New York Times*, 15 December 1996, p. 8CY.

Janes, Barry T. "History and Structure of Public Access Television." *Journal of Film and Video* 39 (Summer 1987): 14–23.

Jeavons, Thomas H. "Raising Funds for Public Libraries: A Current Overview." *New Directions for Philanthropic Fundraising* (Fall 1995): 75–94.

Jessell, Harry A. "Federal Communications Commission Ponders Problems of Cable Reregulation." *Broadcasting* (26 October 1992): 43–44.

Jessup, Lynn. "And Now . . . the News: Weaver Center Program Puts Students on Both Sides of Television Cameras." *News and Record* (Greensboro, NC), 24 October 1990, sec. People and Places, p. 1–2.

Johnson, Allan. "Television's Fringe Has its Say on Cable Access." *Chicago Tribune*, 6 December 1996, sec. 2, p. 1, 6.

Johnson, Fred. "Democracy in the Information Age." *Community Television Review* 16, no. 2 (1993): 6–7.

Johnson, Nicholas, and Gary G. Gerlach. "The Coming Fight for Cable Access." *Yale Review of Law and Social Action* 2 (1972): 217–25.

Kachur, Donald S. *Grantsmanship: Writing Competitive Proposals.* Normal, IL: Illinois State University, 1994.

Kahin, Brian. "The Internet and the National Information Infrastructure." In *Public Access to the Internet.* Ed. Brian Kahlin and James Keller. Cambridge, MA: MIT Press, 1995.

Kaitcer, Cindy R. *Raising Big Bucks: The Complete Guide to Producing Pledge-Based Special Events.* Chicago: Bonus Books, 1996.

Kaniss, Phyllis. *Making Local News.* Chicago: University of Chicago Press, 1991.

Kaniss, Phyllis. *The Media and the Mayor's Race.* Bloomington, IN: Indiana University Press, 1995.

Kaplan, Ann E., ed. *Giving USA 1998, Annual Report on Philanthropy for the Year 1997.* Norwalk, CT: AAFRC Trust for Philanthropy, 1997.

Karimi, Mohammad. *Iranian Television of Dallas: Cultural Issues, Preservation, and Community Formation.* Master's thesis, University of North Texas, 1997. Unpublished.

Karwin, Thomas J. "Fund-raising and Community Access." *Community Television Review* (January/February 1992): 5–6.

Katz, Jesse. "New Episode of Tragedy Strikes a Mother's Crusade." *Los Angeles Times*, 4 April 1992, Home edition, sec. A, p. 1.

Kay, Peg. *Fund Raising for Cable Television Projects.* Washington, DC: Cable Television Information Center, 1974.

Kellman, Laurie. "Public-Access Cable Could Be Censored under a New Law." *The Washington Times*, 20 November 1992, sec. B, p. 8.

Kellner, Douglas. *Television and the Crisis of Democracy.* Boulder, CO: Westview Press, 1990.

Kellner, Douglas. "Public Access Television and the Struggle for Democracy." In *Democratic Communications in the Infomation Age.* Ed. Janet Wasko and Vincent Mosco. Norwood, NJ: Ablex Publishing, 1992.

Kelly, Kathleen S. *Building Fund-Raising Theory: An Empirical Test of Four Models of Practice.* Indianapolis, IN: Indiana University Center on Philanthropy, 1994.

Ketcham, Diane. "Long Island Journal." *New York Times,* 23 September 1990, Final edition, sec. LI, p. 12.

Kids and TV: A Parent's Guide to TV Viewing. Charlotte, NC: Public Affairs Division of Cablevision, n.d., 5.

Kieman, Michael. "To Watch is O.K., but To Air is Divine." *U.S. News and World Report,* (16 October 1989): 112.

Klein, Kim. *Fund Raising for Social Change.* Inverness, CA: Chardon Press, 1994.

Koning, Dirk. "The First Amendment—45 Fightin' Words." *Community Television Review* (November/December 1991): 10–11.

Koning, Dirk. "Tactical Television in Paradiso." *Community Television Review* 16, no. 2 (March/April 1993): 10.

Kotarski, John. "Reporting Election Results Online." *The American City and County, Pittsfield* 113, no. 5 (May 1998): 8.

Kucharski, Carl. "The Long and Winding Road to Columbus." *Community Television Review* (Spring 1991): 6–7.

Kucharski, Carl. "Access: The Rediscovered Country." *Community Media Review* 18, no. 1 (1995): 11.

Kuniholm, Roland. *The Complete Book of Model Fund-Raising Letters.* Englewood Cliffs, NJ: Prentice Hall, 1995.

Lampert, Donna. "Cable Television: Does Leased Access Mean Least Access?" *Federal Communications Law Journal* 44 (1992): 245–84.

Lant, Jeffrey L. *Development Today: A Fund Raising Guide for Nonprofit Organizations.* Rev. 4th ed. Cambridge, MA: JLA Publications, 1990.

LeDuc, John R. "Unbundling the Channels: A Functional Approach to Cable Television Legal Analysis." *Federal Communications Law Journal* 41 (1988): 1–16.

Lee, Bill. "Cable Television: It's 'The People's Television.'" *Greensboro (North Carolina) Daily News* (2 September 1974): sec. B, p. 1.

Lee, Bill. "Cable Television: Simple Idea Turns Wild." *Greensboro (North Carolina) Daily News* (2 September 1974): sec. B, p. 1.

Lee, Bill. "Team Approach Lets Access TV Look Professional," *Greensboro (North Carolina) Daily News,* (21 February 1975): sec. B, p. 1.

Lehman, Ann W. *Fundraising Campaigns: Major Donor, Direct Mail, Corporate and Special Events.* San Francisco: Zimmerman, Lehman & Associates, 1994.

Lewis, T. Andrew. "Access, Advocacy and Democracy: What Will Be?" *Community Television Review* (November/December 1991): 6.

Lewis, T. Andrew. "Access and the First Amendment: What Price Freedom of Expression?" *Community Television Review* (March/April 1993): 1.

Lewis, Wilson C. "Investing More Money in Fund Raising—Wisely." In *Taking Fund Raising Seriously,* Ed. Dwight F. Burlingame and Lamont J. Hulse. San Francisco: Jossey-Bass, 1991. 257–71.

Lichtenberg, Judith. *Democracy and the Mass Media.* New York: Cambridge University Press, 1990.

Liebe, Timothy. "Going Public. Amateur Videos on Public Access Television." *Video Magazine* 18, no. 3 (June 1994): 42.

Lieberman, Lynda Suzanne. "Community Television and the Arts: Austin Style." *Community Television Review* 10, no. 1 (1987): 8–10.

Lloyd, Frank W. "The Federal Communications Commission's Cable Inquiry: An Opportunity to Reaffirm the Cable Act." *Cardozo Arts & Entertainment* 8 (1990): 337–86.

Lombardi, Robert L. "1992 Cable Act: Access Provisions and the First Amendment." *Seton Hall Constitutional Law Journal* 4 (Winter 1993): 163–235.

Lukenbill, W. Bernard. "Eroticized, AIDs-HIV Information on Public-Access Television: A Study of Obscenity, State Censorship and Cultural Resistance." *AIDS Education and Prevention* 10, no. 3 (1998): 229–44.

Lull, James. *Media, Communication, Culture.* New York: Columbia University Press, 1995.

Lutzker, Gary S. "The 1992 Cable Act and the First Amendment: What Must, Must not, and May Be Carried." *Cardozo Arts & Entertainment* 12 (1993): 467–97.

Lynn, David. *More Great Fundraising Ideas for Youth Groups: Over 150 Easy-to-Use Moneymakers that Really Work.* Grand Rapids, MI: Zondervan, 1996.

Lynn, William. *The Fundraising Auction Guide: A Workbook for Non-Profit Organizations.* Birmingham, MI: Heliographis, 1995.

Maddocks, Colin. *A Hundred and One Ways to Raise Money for Your Church or Local Charity.* Knutsford: Albino Services, 1994.

Maiella, James, Jr. "Marijuana Message on Public Access Cable TV Ignites Viewer's Outrage." Los Angeles Times, 13 November 1993, Home edition, sec. A, p. 28.

Margolies, Eliot. "An Ideal Marriage: Access and De Anza College." *Community Television Review* 8, no. 4 (1985): 26–27.

Markey, Edward. "Cable Television Regulation: Promoting Competition in a Rapidly Changing World." *Federal Communications Law Journal* 46 (1993): 1–6.

Mathis, Emily Duncan. *Grant Proposals: A Primer for Writers.* Washington, DC: National Catholic Educational Association, 1994.

McCabe, Bruce. "BNN-TV Wins Top Award for Public-Access Efforts." *Boston Globe,* 6 July 1995, p. 62.

McChesney, Robert W. "Communication for the Hell of It: The Triviality of U.S. Broadcasting History." *Journal of Broadcasting and Electronic Media* 40 (1996): 540–52.

McConnell, Chris. "Cable Backs Public Interest Rules—for DBS." *Broadcasting and Cable* 127, no. 19 (5 May 1997): 21–24.

McConville, Jim. "MTV Makes 'Odd' Talk Choice." *Electronic Media* 16, no. 7 (10 February 1997): 8.

McDonald, Maureen. "It's Showtime: Business Programming Heats up Local Access Channels." *Detroiter* 13, no. 12 (December 1991): 73.

McIntyre, Jerilyn S. "The Hutchins Commission's Search for a Moral Framework." *Journalism History* 6, no. 2 (Summer 1979): 54–63.

McIntyre, Jerilyn S. "Repositioning a Landmark: The Hutchins Commission and Freedom of the Press." *Critical Studies in Mass Communication* 4 (June 1987): 136–60.

McKinley, James C., Jr. "U.S. Court Will Consider a Cable Company's Plan to Scramble a Blue Channel." *New York Times,* 16 September 1995, p. 16.

McLane, Betsy A. "Community Access Cable Television: Use it or Lose it." *Journal of Film and Video* 39 (Summer 1987): 3–4.

McNeil, Alex. *Total Television: A Comprehensive Guide to Programming from 1948 to the Present.* New York: Penguin Books, 1984.

McQuail, Denis. "Mass Media in the Public Interest: Towards a Framework of Norms for Media Performance." In *Mass Media and Society.* Ed. James Curran and Michael Gurevitch. New York: Edward Arnold, 1991.

Meadows, Donella. "Beware of the Right-Leaning Control of the Left-Leaning Media." *News and Record* (Greensboro, North Carolina), 9 April 1995, sec. F, p. 4.

Meiklejohn, Alexander. *Free Speech and its Relation to Self Government.* New York: Harper and Row, 1948.

Merrill, John Calhoun. *The Imperative of Freedom: A Philosophy of Journalistic Autonomy.* New York: Hastings House, 1974.

Meyerson, Michael I. "The Cable Communications Policy Act of 1984: Balancing Act on the Coaxial Wires." *Georgia Law Review* 19 (1985): 543–622.

Meyerson, Michael I. "Cable Television's New Legal Universe: Early Judicial Response to the Cable Act," *Cardozo Arts and Entertainment Law Journal* 6 (1987): 1–36.

Meyerson, Michael I. "Amending the Oversight: Legislative Drafting and the Cable Act." *Cardozo Arts and Entertainment* 8 (1990): 233–55.

Meyerson, Michael I. "Public Access as a High Tech Public Forum." *Community Television Review* (November/December 1991): 8–9.

Miami Herald Publishing Co. v. Tornillo, 418 U.S. 241 (1974).

Mill, John Stuart. *On Liberty, American State Papers.* Ed. R. M. Hutchins. Chicago: William Bennett, 1952.

Miller, James D., and Deborah Strauss, eds. *Improving Fundraising with Technology.* San Francisco: Jossey-Bass, 1996.

Miller, Joyce. "The Development of Community Television," *Community Television Review* 9 (1986): 12.

Miller, Nicholas P., and Alan Beales. "Regulating Cable Television." *Washington Law Review* 57 (1981): 85–86.

Miller, Nicholas P., and Joseph Van Eaton. "A Review of Developments in Cases Defining the Scope of the First Amendment Rights of Cable Television Operators." *Cable Television Law* 2 (1993): 298.

Mininberg, Mark. "Circumstances within our Control: Promoting Freedom of Expression through Cable Television." *Hastings Constitutional Quarterly* 71 (1984): 551–98.

Minner, Joseph S. "Potential Unlimited." *Public Management* (June 1980): 7–8.

"Mission Viejo OKs Cable Channel for Public's Use." *Los Angeles Times,* 1 May 1993, Orange County edition, sec. B, p. 6.

Missouri Knights of the Ku Klux Klan v. City of Kansas City, Missouri, 723 F Supp. 1347 (W.D. Mo. 1989).

Money-Making Ideas for Your Event. Port Angeles, WA: International Festivals Association, 1993.

Morgan, Michael. "Television and Democracy." In *Cultural Politics in Contemporary America.* Ed. Ian Angus and Sut Jhally. New York: Routledge, 1989.

Moss, Mitchell L., and Robert Warren. "Public Policy and Community-Oriented Uses of Cable Television." *Urban Affairs Quarterly* 20 (1984): 233–54.

Muirhead, G.B. "Six Access Channels." *Public Management* (June 1980): 8–9.

Murray, Dennis J. *The Guaranteed Fund-Raising System: A Systems Approach to Developing Fund-Raising Plans*. Poughkeepsie, NY: American Institute of Management, 1994.

National Association of Regulating Utility Commissioners v. Federal Communications Commission, 533 F.2d 601 (1976).

Nauffts, Mitchell F. *Foundation Fundamentals: A Guide for Grantseekers*. New York: Foundation Center, 1994.

Newman, Andy. "More than Television." *New York Times*, 7 January 1996, New Jersey edition, p. 1, 10.

Nichols, Judith E. *Targeted Fund Raising: Defining and Refining Your Development Strategy*. Chicago: Precept Press, 1991.

Nicholson, Margie. "Cable Access: Community Channels and Productions for Nonprofits." *Strategic Communications for Nonprofits*. Washington, DC: Benton Foundation, 1992.

Niemeyer, Suzanne. *Money for Film and Video Artists*. New York: American Council for the Arts, 1991.

"Northern Virginia Youth Services Coalition—NVYSC." *Benton Bulletin* 3 (April 1990): 47–50. *Notice of Inquiry*, 15 FCC 2d. 417 (1968).

Notice of Proposed Rulemaking, 25 FCC 2d 38 (1970).

Ognianova, Ekaterina, and James W. Endersby. "Objectivity Revisited: A Spatial Model of Political Ideology and Mass Communication." *Journalism and Mass Communication Monographs* 159 (October 1996): 1–36.

Olatunji, Sunday O. *Free Money in America and How to Get It*. New York: Olatunji Books, 1994.

O'Neill, Michael J. *The Roar of the Crowd: How Television and People Power are Changing the World*. New York: Times Books, 1993.

Ostrander, Susan A. *Money for Change: Social Movement Philanthropy at Haymarket People's Fund*. Philadelphia: Temple University Press, 1995.

Passingham, Sarah. *Organising Local Events*, 2d ed. London: The Directory of Social Change, 1995.

Payne, Eloise, and Don Derosby. *Using Video: The VCR Revolution for Nonprofits*. Washington, DC: Benton Foundation, 1991.

Payne, Eloise, and Neal Sacharow. *Making Video: A Practical Guide for Nonprofits*. Washington, DC: Benton Foundation, 1993.

Payton, Robert L., Henry A. Rosso, and Eugene R. Tempel. "Toward a Philosophy of Fund Raising." In *Taking Fund Raising Seriously*. Ed. Dwight F. Burlingame and Lamont J. Hulse. San Francisco: Jossey-Bass, 1991. 3–17.

Perry Education Association v. Perry Local Educators' Association, 460 US 37, 45 (1983).

Petrozzello, Donna. "Time Warner Wins NYC Cable News Fight." *Broadcasting and Cable* 127, no. 28 (7 July 1997): 5.

Picard, Robert G. *The Press and the Decline of Democracy: The Democratic Socialist Response in Public Policy*. Westport, CT: Greenwood Press, 1985.

Poderis, Tony. *It's a Great Day to Fund-Raise!: A Veteran Campaigner Reveals the Development Tips and Techniques that Will Work for You*. Cleveland, OH: FundAmerica Press, 1996.

Poe, David R. "As the World Turns: Cable Television and the Cycle of Regulation." *Federal Communications Law Journal* 43 (1991): 141–56.

Polk, Nancy. "The View from New Haven; Public Access TV: It's Storer's Money, but Independent Talent." *New York Times*, 1 May 1994, sec. CN, p. 14.

Porter, Gregory S., and Mark J. Banks. "Cable Access as a Public Forum." *Journalism Quarterly* 65 (1988): 39–45.

Portwood, Pamela. "Renewing the Dream of Access." *Community Television Review* 16, no. 2 (March/April 1993): 8.

Powell, Leilah. *Share Your Success: Fund-Raising Ideas.* Washington, DC: National Trust for Historic Preservation, 1993.

Preferred Communications v. City of Los Angeles, 754 F.2d 1396 (9th Cir. 1985).

Price, Monroe E. "Requiem for the Wired Nation: Cable Rulemaking at the Federal Communications Commission." *Virginia Law Journal* 61 (1975): 541.

Price, Monroe E. *Television, the Public Sphere, and National Identity.* New York: Oxford University Press, 1995.

Price, Monroe E., and John Wicklein. *Cable Television: A Guide for Citizen Action.* Philadelphia: Pilgrim Press, 1972.

"Public Access Cable Show Obscenity Convictions Upheld: Court: 'Safe-Sex' Video not Educational." *News Media and the Law* 20, no. 1 (Winter 1996): 38.

Public, Educational, and Government Access on Cable Television Fact Sheet. Alliance for Community Media, Washington, DC.

Quincy Cable TV v. Federal Communications Commission, 768 F.2d 1434 (1985).

Quinn, Alexander. "Creativity, Diversity and Professionalism in East Multnomah." *Community Television Review* (Spring 1991): 8–9.

Raths, David. "Building Community." *Business Journal* 13 (14 June 1996): 12.

Red Lion Broadcasting, Inc. v. Federal Communications Commission, 395 US 367 (1969).

Rees v. State of Texas, 909 S.W.2d, (Texas Court of Appeals, 3rd District) (1995).

Renstrom, Mary. "Hey, Didn't I See You on Television?" *State Legislatures* 19, no. 6 (1993): 47.

Rice, Jean. "The Communications Pipeline." *Public Management* (June 1980): 2–4.

Rice, Jean. "Cable Television Franchise Renewal: A Practical Guide for Municipal Officials." *New Jersey Municipalities* (November 1988): 16.

Riddle, Anthony. "Prepared Statement of Anthony Riddle, Chair, Alliance for Community Media before the United States Senate." *Federal News Service*, 22 June 1994.

Roberts, Jason. "Public Access: Fortifying the Electronic Soapbox." *Federal Communications Law Journal* 47 (October 1994): 123–52.

Roberts, John. "Cablevision Plans Major Expansion," *Greensboro (North Carolina) Record*, 28 March 1979, sec. A, p. 1, 5.

Roberts, John. "Cablevision: Local Government Decides CG Fate," *Greensboro (North Carolina) Record*, 29 March 1979, sec. A, p. 1, 7.

Roberts, John. "Cable: Quality Programming is Necessary." *Greensboro (North Carolina) Record*, 30 March 1979, sec. A, p. 1, 10.

Robinowitz, Stuart. "Cable Television: Proposals for Reregulation and the First Amendment." *Cardozo Arts and Entertainment* 8 (1990): 309–35.

Roper, Robert St. John. "Unbundling the Channels: A Dysfunctional Aproach to Cable Television Legal Analysis." *Federal Communications Law Journal* 42 (1989): 81–86.

Rosen, Jeffrey. "Cheap Speech." *New Yorker* (7 August 1995): 75–80.

Ross, Jesikah Maria, and J. Aaron Spitzer. "Public Access Television: The Message, the Medium, and the movement." *Art Papers* 18, no. 3 (May/June 1994): 3, 43.

Ross, Stephen R., and Barrett L. Brick. "The Cable Act of 1984—How Did We Get There and Where Are We Going?" *Federal Communications Law Journal* 39 (1986): 27–52.

Rosso, Henry A., ed. *Achieving Excellence in Fund Raising.* San Francisco: Jossey-Bass, 1991.

Rosso, Henry A. "The Philosophy of Fund Raising." In *Achieving Excellence in Fund Raising.* Ed. Henry A. Rosso. San Francisco: Jossey-Bass, 1991.

Rushton, D., Ed. "Citizen Television: A Local Dimension to Public Service Broadcasting." *Institute of Local Television Research Monograph.* London: John Libbey, 1993.

Ruskin, Karen B. *Grantwriting, Fundraising, and Partnerships: Strategies that Work!* Thousand Oaks, CA: Corwin Press, 1995.

Russell, Jim. Whitewater Community Television, Richmond, Indiana. <jarussel@indiana.edu>, Alliance for Community Media Listserv, 31 March 1997, 12:06 PM.

Safire, William. *Safire's Political Dictionary.* New York: Random House, 1978.

Safranek, Thomas W. *Steps for Launching a Capital Campaign.* Washington, DC: National Catholic Education Association, 1996.

Sanchez, Victor. "The Revolving Grant Fund of Manhattan Neighborhood Network." *Community Media Review* 17, no. 2 (March/April 1994): 9.

Saylor, David J. "Municipal Ripoff: The Unconstitutionality of Cable Television Franchise Fees and Access Support Payments." *Catholic University Law Review* 35 (Spring 1986): 673–95.

Saylor, David. "Programming Access and other Competition Regulations of the New Cable Television Law." *Cardozo Arts & Entertainment Journal* 12 (1994): 323–86.

Scannell, Paddy. "For a Phenomenology of Radio and Television." *Journal of Communication* 45, no. 3 (Summer 1995): 4–19.

Schiller, Herbert. "Public Way or Private Road?" *The Nation* 257, no. 21 (12 July 1993): 753.

Schmidt, Benno C. "Freedom of the Press vs. Public Access." *Columbia Law Review* (1976): 15–16.

Schroder, Robert. "Lions Utilize Information Resource." *The Lion Magazine.* (September 1995): 34–35.

Schudson, Michael, *The News Media and the Democratic Process.* New York: Aspen Institute of Humanity Studies, 1983.

Schwartz, Robert. "Public Access to Cable Television." *Hastings Law Journal* 33 (1982): 1009–29.

Schwartz, Tony. *The Responsive Chord.* Garden City, NY: Anchor Press, 1973.

Sclove, Richard E. "Democratizing Technology." *Chronicle of Higher Learning* 12 (January 1994): sec. B, p. 1–2.

Scribner, Susan M. *How to Ask for Money without Fainting: A Guide to Help Nonprofit Staff and Volunteers Raise More Money.* Long Beach, CA: Scribner and Associates, 1992. *Second Report and Order,* 2 FCC 2d 725 (1966).

Seltzer, Michael. *Securing Your Organization's Future.* New York: The Foundation Center, 1987.

Sennett, Richard. *The Fall of Public Man.* New York: Random House, 1972.

Shaffer, D. Scott. "*Preferred Communications, Inc. v. L.A.*: Broadening Cable's First Amendment Rights and Narrowing Cities' Franchising Powers." *Comm/Ent Law Journal* 8 (1986): 535–69.

Shanahan, Dave , and Mary Keyes. "Arts Matter at MATA." *Community Television Review* 10, no. 1 (1987): 13–15, 21.

Shapiro, George H., Philip B. Kurland, and James P. Mercurio. *Cablespeech: The Case for First Amendment Protection.* New York: Harcourt Brace Jovanonich, 1983.

Sharpe, Anita. "Television (A Special Report): What We Watch—Borrowed Time—Public-Access Stations Have a Problem: Cable Companies Don't Want Them Anymore." *Wall Street Journal,* 9 September 1994, Eastern edition, sec. R, p. 12.

Sheldon, K. Scott. "Foundations as a Source of Support." In *Achieving Excellence in Fund Raising.* Ed. Henry A. Rosso. San Francisco: Jossey-Bass, 1991.

Shepard, David S. *How to Fund Media: A Special Project of the Council on Foundations.* Washington, DC: Council on Foundations, 1984.

Shepard, David S. "Media Fund-amentals: Media Can Call Attention to an Issue like Nothing Else: Here's What You Need to Know about Funding Film and Video." *Foundation News* (January/February 1989): 58–61.

Shepard, David S. "A Producer's Potential." *Foundation News* (March/April 1989): 60–62.

Shepard, David S. "Judging Media Budgets." *Foundation News* (May/June 1989): 62–65.

Shepard, David S. "Distribution Solution." *Foundation News* (July/August 1989): 62–65.

Sherman, Kathy. "Information at the Touch of a Button: A Profile of Southfield's Municipal Channel." *Community Television* Review 8, no. 3 (1985): 18.

Sibary, Scott. "The Cable Communications Policy Act of 1984 v. the First Amendment." *Comm/Ent Law Journal* 7 (1985): 381–415.

Siebert, Fred S., Theodore Peterson, and Wilbur Schramm. *Four Theories of the Press.* Urbana: University of Illinois Press, 1963.

Silverman, Fran. "News and Advice on TV for Haitians in the State." *New York Times,* 19 January 1992, Final edition, sec. CN, p. 12.

Sinel, N. M., P. J. Grant, and M. B. Bierut. "Cable Franchise Renewals: A Potential Minefield." *Federal Communications Law Journal* 39 (1986): 77–107.

Sinel, N. M., P. J. Grant, C. H. Little, and W. E. Cook. "Current Issues in Cable Television: Re-Balancing to Protect the Consumer." *Cardozo Arts & Entertainment* 8 (1989): 387–402.

Smith, Becky. *How to Raise the Money You Need, Now!: Even if There's not Enough Staff, Money, or Time for Fund Raising.* Tulsa, OK: National Resource Center for Youth Services, 1992.

Smith, George Harmon. *How to Write Winning Grant Proposals.* RMS Publishing, 1995.

Smith, Jane. "The People's Channel." *Independent Weekly,* 16 November 1995, p. 21.

Sparks, Colin. "The Press, the Market, and Democracy." *Journal of Communication* (winter 1992): 36–51.

Special Events Fundraising: A Guide for Nonprofits. Richmond, KY: The Council, 1992.

Spence, Holly. "Project VITAL." *Community Television Review* 10, no. 2 (1987): 16–17.

Splichal, Slavko, and Janet Wasko. *Communication and Democracy.* Norwood, NJ: Ablex Publishing, 1993.

Stanton, Martha, and Wendy Wilson. "Making the Most of Cable Television Technology." *T.H.E. Journal* (May 1992): 67–69.

Stark, Ben. "At HOM(e) in Meridan Township." *Community Television Review* (Spring 1991): 10–11.

Steinglass, David Ehrenfest, "Extending *Pruneyard*: Citizens' Right to Demand Public Access Cable Channels," *New York University Law Review* 71 (October 1996): 1160.

Stern, Christopher. "Nudity Clause Gives Cable Operators Pause." *Broadcasting and Cable* 55 (17 April 1995): 4–17.

Stoneman, Donnell. "D.I.Y. Television." *News and Record* (Greensboro, North Carolina), 12 May 1992, sec. D, p. 1.

Strauss, Neil. "At 18, the 'Squirt TV' Guy Resumes his Pop-Scene Assault." *New York Times*, 9 September 1997, sec. C, p. 9.

"Structural Regulations of Cable Television: A Formula for Diversity." *Communication and Law* 15 (1993): 43–70.

Sturken, Marita. "An Interview with George Stoney." *Afterimage* (January 1984): 7–12.

Szykowny, Rick. "The Threat of Public Access: An Interview with Chris Hill and Brian Springer." *The Humanist* 54 (1994): 15–23.

"TCI Cable Makes Official Cutback in Public Access." *New York Times*, 7 April 1996, sec. WC, p. 13.

Telecommunications Act of 1996, U.S. Code Supplement II, vol. 47, sec. 531–59 (1996).

Treistman, Peter, and Sam Behrend. "Transformal and Expansion at Tucson." *Community Television Review* (Spring 1991): 10.

Turner Broadcasting System, Inc. v. FCC, 512 US 1145 (1994).

Turner Broadcasting System, Inc. v. FCC, 117 SCt 1174 (1997).

Turner, Richard C. "Metaphors Fund Raisers Live by: Language and Reality in Fund Raising." In *Taking Fund Raising Seriously*, Ed. Dwight F. Burlingame and Lamont J. Hulse. San Francisco: Jossey–Bass, 1991.

"21st Century Production Facilities." *Video Letter* 1, no. 7 (fall 1988): 1–3.

United States v. Midwest Video, 406 U.S. 649 (1972).

United States v. Midwest Video Corporation, 406 US 649 (1979).

United States v. O'Brien, 391 U.S. 367 (1968).

United States v. Southwestern Cable Co., 392 U.S. 157 (1968).

vanEijk, Nico. "Freedom of Expression in Europe: Just Forty Years." *Community Television Review* 13 (November/December 1991): 13.

Vanamee, Norman. "Eat Drink Man Lizard." *New York* (11 November 1996): 20, 22.

Vickroy, Thelma. "Live from Norwalk: How One City Saved Community Programming." *Journal of Film and Video* 39 (Summer 1987): 24–27.

Vinsel, Deborah. "Community People, Community Access." *Community Media Review* 19, no. 4 (1996): 9, 12, 13.

Visser, Randy. "South Portland; Where Video Meets the Sea." *Community Television Review* (Spring 1991): 7–8.

Wadlow, R. Clark, and Linda M. Wellstein. "The Changing Regulatory Terrain of Cable Television." *Catholic University Law Review* 35 (1986): 705–36.

Walker, Bonnie L. "Community Access Television Fills a Need in Bowie." *Community Television Review* 10, no. 1 (1987): 22–23.

Ward, Jean. "Connect with Cable Television." *Library Journal* (July 1992): 38–41.

Warwick, Mal. *How to Write Successful Fundraising Letters*. Berkeley, CA: Strathmoor Press, 1994.

Warwick, Mal. *The Hands-On Guide to Fundraising Strategy and Evaluation*. Gaithersburg, MD: Aspen Public, 1995.

Washburn, Jim. "Crean's World; Spiders in the Salad! Towels Aflame! This is Cooking—on Local Cable, of Course." *Los Angeles Times*, 25 May 1993, Home edition, sec. E, p. 1.

Webb, William. "Public Interest Journalism in the Online Era." *Editor and Publisher* 128, no. 23 (10 June 1995): 28.

Webster, Bernard R. *Access: Technology and Access to Communication Media*. Paris: Unesco Press, 1975.

Wedlin, Wayne. "The Essential Element." *Public Management* (June 1980): 9–10.

Wenker, John H. "Provisions of Cable Services since Deregulation & Proposals for Reregulation or Elvis is Alive and Well on Cable Ch. 54, But How Much Will it Cost to Watch Him?" *Hamline Journal of Public Law* 12 (1991): 341–58.

White, Christopher F. "Eye on the Saprrow: Community Access Television in Austin, Texas." Ph.D. diss., The University of Texas at Austin, 1988.

Williams, Frederick, and John V. Pavlik, eds. *The People's Right to Know: Media Democracy, and the Information Highway*. Hillsdale, NJ: L. Erlbaum Associates, 1994.

Williams, Warrene. *User Friendly Fund$raising: A Step-by-Step Guide to Profitable Special Events*. Alexander, North Carolina: WorldComm, 1994.

Winn, Debra Maldon *Six Easy Steps to $$Millions$$ in Grants: A Grant-Writing Manual*. El Cerrito, CA: Maldon Enterprise, 1993.

Winner, Langdon. "Artifact/Ideas and Political Culture." *Community Television Review* 16, no. 2 (March/April 1993): 16.

Wright, Jeff, Katherine Lima, and Dotti Wilson, "Fund-Raising Fundamentals." *Community Television Review*. (January/February 1992): 9–13.

"You Oughta Be on Television." *Modern Maturity Magazine* (June/July 1991): 48–50.

Young, Theresa. "Public Access Reaching the Community through Cable TV." *FBI Law Enforcement Bulletin* 66, no. 6 (June 1997): 20–27.

"Youth Get in Focus at Cable Access of Dallas." *Community Television Review* 15 (1991): 15.

Zeiger, Dinah. "TCI Goes Live to Keep Customers Sweet." *The Denver Post*, 30 January 1995, sec. C, p. 1.

Zimmerman, Robert M. *Grantseeking: A Step-by-Step Approach*. San Francisco: Zimmerman, Lehman, 1994.

Index

benefit rationale, 52
Benton Foundation, 39
BET, 46, 47
"Biograph Days, Biograph Nights," 42
black power, 10, 11
Boninfante, Lenora, 47
"Bonjour," 38
Boston, MA, 3, 8, 37
Boston Community Television, 37
Boston Globe, 46
Boulder, CO, 23
Brattleboro, VT, 9
Brattleboro (Vermont) Community
    Television, 9
Briller, Bert, 80
broadcast television compared to cable,
    24 Table 2.1
Broadway, 42
Brockton, MA, 41
Brooklyn, NY, 9
Brooklyn Public Access Corporation, 9
Bucks County, PA, 40
Buell, Glendora, 42
bulletin board, 9, 65; and hate messages,
    10–11; instead of programming,
    37, 38; and self-promotion, 74;
    underwriting, 60
Burlington, VT, 38
Burns, Red, 5–7
Bush, George, 12
Buttafucco, Joey, 43

Cable Access, 39
Cable Communications Policy Act of
    1984, 8, 11–12, 26–27, 51–52;
    differences with Cable Act of
    1992, 27–28; six purposes of, 26
cable company, 31, 51, 53; and competi-
    tion with other cable companies,
    9; and editorial control, 27,
    29–30, 55–56; and franchise fees,
    51; grants from, xxvii, 53; and
    indecency, 29; and must carry, 26,
    28; and public access, xxviii, 5,
    73, 79–80; and public access man-
    agement, 35–36, 44; and public

rights of way, 23; subscribers,
    number of, 51
cable franchise, 6, 9, 11, 30, 31
cable industry, 9; deregulation of, xxvii;
    as public access television advo-
    cate, 8
cable television: Canadian Policy
    Statement on, 4; compared to
    broadcast television, 24; and FCC
    regulation of, 22; potential of, 18;
    and public access requirements,
    28; and studies of awareness of
    public access television, 46 Table
    3.3; viewership, 47 Table 3.4
*Cable Television Consumer Protection
    and Competition Act of 1992*, 12,
    27–30, 31; and public access
    requirements, 28; and must-carry,
    28; and DBS (direct broadcast
    satellite), 28; objectives of, 27–28;
    and obscenity on PEG or leased
    access, 28–29
*Cable Television Report and Order of
    1972*, 7, 20; of 1976, 22
Cable TV, Inc., 6
Cablevision of New Jersey, 36
"Cafe with Andre," 42
Caldicott, Helen, 10
California, 5, 11, 37, 40, 43, 67
call-in shows, 38–39, 40–41
CAN TV (Chicago Access Network),
    xxv, 41
Canadian National Film Board, 3
Canadian Radio and Television
    Commission, policy statement on
    cable television, 4
Cape May County, NJ, 47
capital campaign, 55, 56, 60
Carmichael, Stokeley (Kwame Ture), 10
"Catch 44," 3
CATV (Community Antenna Television),
    17
"Caviar & Grits," 41
CBN, 46, 47
CBS, 35
CD-ROM disks, 41
Challenge for Change, 1, 3, 4

About the Author

LAURA R. LINDER is an Assistant Professor in the Broadcasting/Cinema and Theatre Department at the University of North Carolina at Greensboro. Her articles appear in *The History of Mass Media in the United States* and she was one of the founders of Greensboro Community Television and is a member of the Southeast Board of Directors of the Alliance for Community Media.